Inside the Family Business

Inside the
Family Business

Léon A. Danco

THE CENTER FOR FAMILY BUSINESS

university press, inc.

Post Office Box 24268
Cleveland, Ohio 44124

Library of Congress Cataloging in Publication Data

Danco, Léon A. 1923-
  Inside the family business.

    1. Family corporations—Management. 2. Small
business—Management. I. Title.
HD62.7.d36   658'.022   80-23512
ISBN 0-9603614-1-3

First Printing: September 1980
Second Printing: November 1980

Printed in USA

Contents

"In His wisdom God gives to each of us a limited, finite number of hours a year in which to achieve our goals, both material and spiritual. He gives us these hours in sequence, day by day, month by month. If they are wasted, however, they are neither repeatable nor refundable. He gives the same amount to the rich and to the poor, to the young and to the old. Whatever successes we may achieve in this life will come from the purpose to which we put God's priceless gift — *time.*"

Léon A. Danco, Ph.D.

Acknowledgements

Writing books is a lot like raising children or starting businesses--success is always a delight and surprise (it's awesome to realize that God gives children to inexperienced parents). What could we accomplish if only we knew what we were doing?

With second children, or second businesses, (and, of course, even second books) we think at first that we really know what we're doing. What we eventually realize, however, is how lucky we were the first time. If we're wise, we gratefully accept all the help we can find.

INSIDE THE FAMILY BUSINESS is such a second creation. While I can take responsibility for its existence, it would be ignoble of me, if not downright insensitive and ungrateful, if I were not to mention the tremendous assistance and insight and encouragement given to me by my wife, Katy, and our children.

They have helped me understand more clearly than ever how grateful a successful business owner must be both to his mate of nearly 30 years and to the fruit of their union, not only for their support, but for their contribution to his dreams.

I also owe a huge debt of gratitude to our dedicated directors for their contribution to The Center for Family Business, to the outstanding faculty of our continuing Seminars for the Business Owner and his Family, and to the participants in those seminars--both men and women, founders and inheritors--all of whom have so generously shared with me their insights and their faith in the family business as a defender of free enterprise and their hope for its future.

Finally as a teacher, I wish especially to acknowledge my special appreciation to my finest student, Donald Jonovic, without whose collaboration and contribution this book would probably not exist.

L.A.D.

Preface

This book is written for winners, not losers. I don't know what to say to chronic complainers, malcontents or the incompetant. I really don't understand them or their world.

The world I know and understand is the world of those well-adjusted, fundamentally happy, positive people who have succeeded in struggling their lonesome way up the rough ladder called "my own business." This book is about them and those people who are following them up that ladder--their heirs and successors.

INSIDE THE FAMILY BUSINESS means just what it says. I want you to come with me inside one of the most exciting worlds I know. You're going to meet all kinds of people in that world, some you know, some you don't know, and even a few you wish you didn't know. You might even meet yourself here and there, and what you see won't always be all that comfortable. But this world has to be understood to ensure that a successful family business *can* continue, generation after generation.

I see far too many of the winners *losing* in the end. I see far too many great men and women whose dreams and work over many hard years come to ashes, whose *successful* family-owned businesses fail to last much past the first generation. The only way this trend can be reversed is by developing an understanding of what a successful business invariably requires in commitment, compassion, and contribution.

It's true that the business owner is confused, misinterpreted, harrassed, over-reactive, and feels very alone. But his problems don't exist in a vacuum. If anything, they will only be amplified by his unwitting, but self-imposed isolation.

Many other people, however, add to and share his problems. The family business can sometimes be a world of wives who don't understand or seem to care, of kids who won't work to their father's standards, of fathers who don't or won't understand their children or their mates. It can also contain some family members whose selfishness negates their contribution to the whole, and former friends filled with envy at the business owner's rapid rise in socio-economic status.

These problems are often ignored or sometimes even fostered by self-serving advisors who become gladiators in their own right. These problems are often amplified by self-anointed "directors" who see their mission only as assuring their own selfish well-being.

And, as if these forces weren't enough. we also live in an economic world characterized by taxation, inflation, excessive government regulation, and the indifference of labor.

All of these people and facts add to an unbelievable pressure on the business owner, a pressure often compounded by inarticulateness, undisciplined greed, and the total absence of contribution or compassion. It seems more and more a rarity that the business family understands that their family business is a package deal, that burdens go with privilege.

But the business owner brings most of this on himself. He has difficulty being understood by his contemporaries, his peers, his subordinates, and by everybody else--including his family. He finds it very difficult to state his opinions clearly and honestly. He's not willing, in general, to be vulnerable to other people's criticisms of his decisions, his ideas, and his methods.

Instead, he chooses to pretend the silence following his non-negotiable pronouncements means he's "being understood." Instead of expressing his strong opinions articulately and opening himself up to the possibility of criticism by people who might have a valid difference of opinion, he bellows like an outraged orangutan or preaches like a pompous pedant. Everyone else is expected to nod, bite their tongues, and swallow their opinions.

Most of what happens to his business in the future is in his lap. He is, after all, the occupant of the throne. Most of what must happen, he must initiate. But his family, his managers, and his contemporaries must share the responsibility for the continuity of that business. This is why a book about the family business cannot be written without taking this wider world into account.

Without communication, the business owner and his family are on different horses, riding off into separate sunsets, while the business stumbles along like a mule with blinders--tunnel-visioned and sterile.

Business owners and their families deserve better than this.

The business owner's dream that his business continue from generation to generation isn't only understandable. It's also possible. There's really no reason why the business owner should fail. Help is available. It's available through the support of his family, his heirs, and his carefully chosen directors, advisors, and managers. Help is available through sincere association with his peers, through better education and organization of his management. Help is available because the upgrading of the quality and commitment of those involved in the business is possible.

But this help from others depends on the business owner. It depends on his willingness and ability to learn, accept, and understand the emotional and technical facts which will enable him to provide the initiative for the continued well being of what he has created.

I believe that life in a successful, humane, and growing family business is among the best ways of life society has yet devised...and that this life is possible, given commitment, understanding, love, and the most competent professional help the business environment has to offer.

The encouragement of vital, healthy family-owned businesses has been my dedication for over 20 years. It should be the goal of every business professional, of government, of the public corporation, and, most important, of *all* the people involved in the family business itself.

Because I believe so strongly that the survival and growth of America's privately-held family-owned businesses are the keys to the future of our country, I dedicate this book to our children and our grandchildren... yours and mine.

It is, after all, mainly for them and their tomorrows that we are building today.

Léon A. Danco, Ph.D.

Cleveland, Ohio

Introduction

Everything cometh to him who waiteth,
If while he waiteth he worketh like hell.

We were sitting on the beach in Hawaii one day, telling war stories in the shade of a tall palm. He was a first-class guy, my age, an ex-marine. He'd gone through all the campaigns in the Southwest Pacific and came out a combat hero. He was ambitious, talented, well-educated, hardnosed, and hard working.

In the 30-plus years that had passed between the end of the war and our conversation on the beach, he had founded and built a great business, with a couple hundred employees, a competent management and an accepted product line. His business was well organized and profitable. His future seemed, by any standard, to be well assured.

As he looked out over the Pacific, he told me quietly that he had only a few months left. He said we probably wouldn't be meeting again because he wouldn't be around. The years had taken their toll. He had drunk too much, smoked too much, stayed out too late. He had destroyed his body. And then he told me something I will never forget: "You know," he said, "If I'd known I was going to live this long, I would have taken better care of myself."

Why is it that we never think the future will come to pass? We never think that our hair will thin, that our gut will expand, or that our children will grow up? Why do we get so surprised when we find our blood pressure rising and our energy lessening? Why are we shocked when success brings us more problems than it solves? We become surprised by the obvious. All of these things invariably come to pass and when they do, we shake our heads and share regrets. The future happens eventually to every one of us.

Now that I'm at the age where what was once my future is now my present, and now that I've had the privilege to meet tens of thousands of successful business owners and study the inner workings of many thousands of family-owned businesses, I have a new perspective on these businesses, a perspective related to both past and future.

THE IMPORTANCE OF TIME

A family-owned business can only be understood over time. Like trees, whose rings can tell what kinds of struggles the growing plant went through, the family business as it is today is foreshadowed by all that went before. What exists today is the substance out of which tomorrow's business will grow. This is why a plan for the future, based on the past as well as the present, must be built if any useful change is to occur.

Family businesses are unique because they are composed of a flow through time of people with conflicting needs, concerns, abilities, and rights--who also share one of the strongest bonds human beings can have, a family relationship.

The family-owned business is so much more than just a business. It's a stew of family relationships, based both on love and on resentment. It's a mixture of opportunity and entitlement--heavily masked by the more obvious ingredients of jobs, money, taxes, products, markets, and benefits. No wonder it has a tendency to boil over.

THE IMPORTANCE OF THE FAMILY

The vast majority of what is written today under the general heading of business management deals with *technique* --methods to manage this or organize that, to invest here or divest there, how to escape, minimize, or defer taxes, how to enlarge markets or cut costs, how to stop the unions or how to motivate the employees. But our intimate knowledge of the *insides* of family-owned businesses makes it increasingly obvious that it is the *concerns of the family* which are at the base of the family business, and which absorb most of the owner-manager's time and energy--too often at the expense of pressing business needs.

The energies a business owner will need for success in the coming decade will be taxed to their utmost if he is successfully to guide his business through the perils of inflation, taxation, regulations, shortages, unemployment, energy and other crises. But if the family problems are not solved, the owner will not have enough energy to solve these problems.

Too high a price will be paid by business owners for not facing up to the facts as they become known. There is just so much human energy and only one concern at a time can have first priority in our mind and in our attention. Publicly owned companies manage to succeed despite their general lack of the entrepreneur's vision and tenacity, and despite all the adversities--job shifts, personnel changes, bureaucracy--inherent in the larger organization, because what little energy they have available goes *on the job* , to solve the vital problems of business survival in an increasingly complex world.

Too often, what energy there is available to the successful family business is absorbed fighting thousands of needless little brush wars and skirmishes among the family members. Must these battles occur? Can't we give peace a chance?

THE RUNNING SANDS

Too often, because we're caught in the short term putting out today's fires, we don't take the time to think about this thing called the family business and about the future--the future both of the business and of all the people involved in it. We are too often obsessed with fighting the unions, beating Uncle Sam, keeping the employees off our backs, selling customers and cutting costs, all the daily crises that keep us from finding the time to think about *tomorrow* and giving *it* the time it requires.

It's true that this kind of tunnel vision is what brings success in the early days of a business, but, for the family in business, market and financial success is only the beginning. In fact, it is only one of the middle stages in an involved and complicated process.

And that process is severely constricted by *time* --more specifically, by lifetimes.

A lifetime, even one that's longer than average, is at most only 1000 months long. That would take us from birth to a little over 83 years of age. We each begin at zero and we each have a certain finite quota of months assigned to us by the Eternal Accounting Department. My grandson, for example, has already chewed up 50 of his 1000 months, and his little sister is working on her 30th month. I've gone through almost 700 of mine. My children are already half my age.

And short as 1000 months may seem, it's longer than the *useful* lifetime most of us have. If we look at our actual *contributory* lifetime, even assuming we begin doing positive and useful things fairly early, those 83 years can be reduced to 75. That's only 900 months. Yet, in that short time, we have three major responsibilities--all independent of what we are actually accomplishing.

THE LEARNING YEARS

In our first 300 months, we *learn* and we *consume*. We learn who we are. We learn to count on our fingers, we learn to go to school, we chase the opposite sex. We learn to ride bicycles and take photographs, to climb trees and play games. In those first 25 years we are primarily learners and consumers, and our contribution to society, other than giving joy to our parents, is fairly minimal.

My thinking about these years probably coincided with the arrival of my grandchildren. Like most business owners, I was too busy to watch my own children grow up, but now I have the luxury of watching my grandchildren. They live in my home town and we see them most days when we're home. Those little people haven't any idea what they're supposed to do, but they're learning and learning fast. Like all of us, they are going to continue to learn more, to go off to school, to learn about themselves, the world, and its people.

This is the time every one of us uses to acquire the skills and knowledge we need to live in our world. It is during these first 25 years that we pick up most of the attitudes and opinions, images and memories that will guide us in the future. We also gain impressions from our parents and from our grandparents, and because of this we are more reflective of our grandparents than most of us realize.

A family business, because it so closely reflects the character and personality of the owner-founder, has a great deal of the business owner's early years built into it--even though he and his partners don't usually realize it.

The mysterious chemistry of the entrepreneur is a mixture of subtle influences: whether he was raised in poverty or affluence, whether he was raised as one of many children or as an only child, whether he came from a large and loving family, or whether he was orphaned at an early age, etc., etc. All of an almost infinite number of factors make up the qualities absorbed in our first 25 years, and those qualities, without any doubt, continue to have a great influence on the way we proceed in our remaining years.

THE DOING YEARS

Of course we never really stop learning, but at some point around our 25th birthday or so, we've usually made our choice of mate, and probably have settled into some kind of occupation. We've found the place we want to live. Our education--in the formal sense--is completed. We begin to do things. Some things we do well. Some we do badly. We win, we lose. We get fired, we quit, we get thrown out, we change. But we begin to *do* , to *produce* , to make whatever positive contribution we are going to make.

This is forced on us by life. We take the jagged, precarious climb upwards through our individual curves because we must--those of us, at least, who choose not to drop out. We must learn and we must do. In this process we accumulate experiences--good and bad, valid and invalid--we impose our views on others--as others impose their views on us.

Whatever contribution most of us make in our lives, this is the time we do it--during our *productive years* with our mates, our children, our careers.

By 50, most of our accomplishments are apparent, whatever they may be, and we're about to enter our last contributory 300 months. By the time we enter our fifties, we've been at it a long time, longer than we'd care to remember. We're a little tired of the struggle, the never-ending day to day battles, and we'd mostly just like to coast for a while. We'd like to reap the rewards of all of our struggles. What happens is we approach another fundamental decision, only this one is *not* forced on us.

This is the point where we begin pleading: "God, I don't want any more. I just want to keep what I have and enjoy it." Sometimes this is more of an inward or unadmitted expression. To the outside world we say we never felt better--but in reality that precious mixture of guts, creativity, drive and need don't really repeat themselves--we mostly just kid ourselves and indulge our youthful image with more expensive toys because we can afford them, pontificate in front of people we pay to applaud, and exercise our "muscle" without the discipline that was imposed by the more Spartan circumstances of our earlier days.

At this time in our lives as business owners, we begin to have daydreams of collecting our receivables faster than we post them. We have visions of turning our inventory over at an ever faster rate, and having our capital reinvestment become less than our depreciation.

We want to have lunch with our banker, to turn our assets into cash, and to vote Republican with a clear conscience. All the good things--and we dream of carrying them off into some permanent sunset. What we want is peace, quiet, enjoyment, and love--and we think we deserve it. Sometimes we cover up for this lack of accomplishment by a flurry of activities in marginally useful areas--which is not that hard to do.

If the golden goose can just keep producing those golden eggs, we only have to rationalize our activities to justify them. If we can afford them--our toys become more exotic. Of course they remain deductible.

THE TEACHING YEARS

But it isn't all that simple. A new generation is born every 25 years or so. And this new generation goes through the same process of learning that the previous generation did. While Dad was going through his doing and producing years, his years from 25 to 50, a *new* generation was consuming and learning. But consider what he and they were learning.

> *This is probably as good a place as any to explain the*
> *masculine bias in my English and in this book. I grew*
> *up in a male-dominated world and the great majority of*
> *successful business owners today are males. The same is*
> *true--though on a steadily decreasing scale--of their*
> *successors. My knowledge and experience was gained in*
> *this world, but this should not be taken to mean that I*
> *ignore or minimize the role of women. It's just that I*
> *haven't had enough experience with female entrepreneurs*
> *to feel that I can speak knowledgeably about them.*
> *Women today are becoming increasingly involved in*
> *family businesses as owners and managers, an*
> *involvement I welcome greatly. Where my English seems*
> *to slight that increasing role, however, the blame properly*
> *lies with the language. English never got around to*
> *inventing genderless pronouns other than "it," and the*
> *constant use of he/she, him/her, or even son/daughter in*
> *a manuscript this long would drive us all to distraction.*
> *I beg your forebearance...and forgiveness. But please,*
> *Ladies, let me include you as "one of the boys."*

Because lifetimes overlap, dads are *doing* when the kids are *learning*, and what the kids learn is often a shame. They watch Daddy--very carefully--and they listen to him when he unwittingly poisons them about the business that has placed so many demands on him. Ever wonder why the kids are less than enthusiastic? Dad's been discouraging them from the beginning.

The kids grow up during Dad's *doing* years, the years when more was better, the years when he spent so much time away from home that when he finally did walk in the door, the dog bit him and the kids wondered who was kissing their mother.

This is why there must be a third concurrent and residual career called *teaching* , which completes a spiral of all the generations. The family business must be a migration of these interactive generations into the future, not merely one generation repeated many times.

This realization comes to us not only by observation, but by experience as well. I, too, am now a grandfather approaching the end of my doing phase. I watch my grandchildren watching their parents, as my children must have watched me, and as I watched my parents and grandparents. I realize now that *our* future depends upon what *they* see and what they learn from me.

THE CENTER OF FIVE GENERATIONS

A successful family business involves the lives, hopes, dreams, and effort of five generations--the founder being only the middle generation. Unless positive teaching between the generations occurs, the spiral will probably break, possibly forever. I've had too many phone calls from too many men my age who said to me, "I don't know what to do with my children. They want no part of our family business--they've seen what their grandfather has done to me."

Don't think this thought doesn't rattle my own cage. My grandchildren are getting their picture of what their world is going to be by watching me and their father. I thought I was watching them--but no, they're watching me, just as there was a time when my father was in my position and my children were watching what their grandfather and father did. It's a continuum, a circle.

We must follow the progress of the family business through time as a process of multiple generations which are cumulatively learning, doing, and teaching--with teaching serving as the phase that links the generations in succession and continuity.

The failure to teach--or the unwillingness to learn--are two of the most dangerous mistakes made in family businesses and are among the primary points of difference between the family managed, privately owned company and the professionally managed publicly owned corporation, where teaching of successive generations of managers is essentially institutionalized.

In the public corporation, teachers are chosen by a selection process that emphasizes articulateness and rewards successful teachers with increasingly more challenging assignments. In the public corporation, students are chosen on the basis of competitive selection, and taught subjects they choose themselves.

In private companies, selection is by accident, teaching by osmosis, and authority by clout. Why can't the family owned business absorb some of the qualities of management instead of using "we're not General Motors" as the answer to all new ideas.

It's a shame that teaching and learning in the family business is sometimes too similar to that in third-rate universities, where the teachers are often not so much qualified as they are kept on by tenure. In these situations, students aren't going to become very motivated.

So, too often in the family business the "student" hangs around, disillusioned and frustrated, supported and trapped by a "scholarship" called "salary." And even this support is not based on merit. It's too often a function of our desire to get even with the Internal Revenue Service because the kids' allowances can now be made deductible.

It's because I've been able to meet so many wonderful heirs (after all everybody is somebody's kid, why do only *ours* have to be no damn good?) that I know that successors *can* be ready and willing to take responsibility. Our job is to prepare them for it and then to prepare ourselves.

A family business is so much more than the sum of technical management techniques within a specific product/service/market concept. An added complexity all too often ignored by most students of business, the press, public corporations, government, and most so-called consultants is that it is a business of *people*. Schools of management are only beginning to notice this special, fundamental difference between the publicly owned and the privately held company.

The difference is a difference in people. The business owner, throughout his "doing" phase is surrounded by people in various relationships, doing various things with him, to him, about him, and sometimes around him. All of these relationships have an effect, good or bad, on the business.

The business owner must not only contend with his managers, his suppliers, his customers, and his competitors, he must also deal with his family. And his children, the next generation, are sitting on the sidelines. They have their own relationships within the business owner's "business" family, as well as with their own brothers, sisters, and cousins. They also interact with their business cousins--the children of their fathers' partners, or those of their key employees and corporate advisors. What are they doing? Are they really helping?

This business family is very complex, and it gets more complex as the years go by. As all the children become adults, we have also to consider the problem of the "instant family," in particular the daughters-in-law, the sons-in-law, uncles, aunts, the children of divorce and remarriage and the changes of heart that so often occur when wives become widows. And to these we have to add the ambitions each has for his own.

These concerns are not minor. The survival of a family business is not just dependent on Ol' Dad or his successors. It's not just dependent on his partners, his creditors, his advisors, the government, or the IRS. It's very dependent, as well, on the women in his family--his wife, his daughters, his sisters, his nieces, and these same women in the lives of his children and his partners.

THE NEED FOR DECISION...AND ACTION

Once the *pressures of the passage of time* are really understood, and the reality of an *extended family* are listed and put in their proper places in the past and future of the business, another major theme begins to emerge. A question naturally arises. Since, 1) we can see how much *time* we have and, 2) we can understand all these *people* with their needs and expectations, now 3) *what do we do?*

What we must do is *decide* --and *act* .

The facts must be recognized. The business has needs and it offers opportunities, but only if the future is constantly and carefully considered. The passage of time is a "fact." The people who are involved in the business and in the family are "facts." The abilities, ambitions, and energies these people have, their desires and demands, all are "facts." What all of these facts together imply is that *something must be done that is consistent with them*.

Too often, I become involved with family businesses late in the founder's life, after many bad decisions have already been made. The passage of time is usually not noticed until it's almost too late. The people and their needs aren't understood. Some children don't want to come into the business, but they're being waited for. Common stock has been given to people who have no continuing contribution to make to the business. Responsibilities have been given out without regard to talent. Estate plans are either based on emotion or, at best, are out of date. Changes in health, or interest, or circumstances are ignored.

The earlier errors can be faced and acted upon, the more likely it will be that the inevitable problems can be solved. It is a fact that if errors have been made, correcting them is going to have to take something out of somebody's hide. Surgery is never without side effects. The earlier the facts are faced, and the treatment decided upon, the less severe those side effects will be.

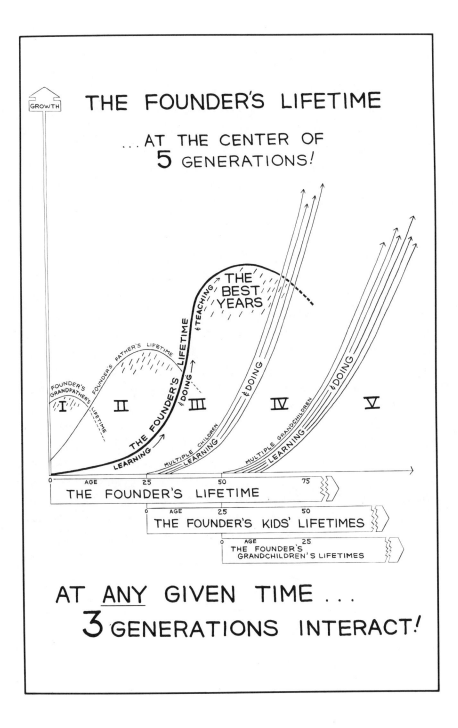

THIS BUSINESS CAN CONTINUE

A family business is a *process* . There are complex relationships among many *people* . These relationships happen through *time* . And through this time, there are *decisions* that are required of the participants.

The real demands, the real skills required by a family business arise from the interaction of these three major ingredients. They must be understood. At each level, and through time, the right actions must be performed if the full potential of a family business is to be realized.

But it's not that easy. Even if the spirit is willing, the flesh is usually weak, and reaching the best of all possible solutions for any given family business may require more understanding than most of us have. But this is part of the dream--that our businesses *will* continue beyond us, carried on by the resources and commitment of those who are prepared for--and accept--the responsibility. The only other option is to assume we are immortal, because without qualified successors, we're going to have to do it all ourselves, and we're going to have to do it forever--or at least as long as we want the business to last.

If only we could be both immortal and celibate. Then this book would not be needed. But we don't live forever and we do have heirs for whom we have dreams. The hourglass sits on the mantle for each of us and each of us can see that all of the sand is no longer at the top. The sand is running. Time is passing. We can't "save" time--we can only invest it while we watch it go by. The best we can all hope for is that while time is passing, what happens is good.

If our Creator is kind to us, the amount of sand in the hourglass is enough for us to do what we have to do, but it's an unknown amount. It is finite and it is running out. And it is not renewable.

Let us study the family business from the birth of the dream through the rebirth of that dream with the heirs. Let us study the process to increase our understanding of what is happening, what has happened, what could happen, and what *should* happen.

Too often, families grow up unprepared for their management and ownership role. Too often we act as though there will be no future. When decisions are made, too often they are bad decisions, made in haste, with little thought given to their consequences tomorrow.

In the family business, as in most human endeavors, it is true that the past is prologue. We must act *now* for our success in the future.

As a very wise man once said, "Chance favors the prepared mind."

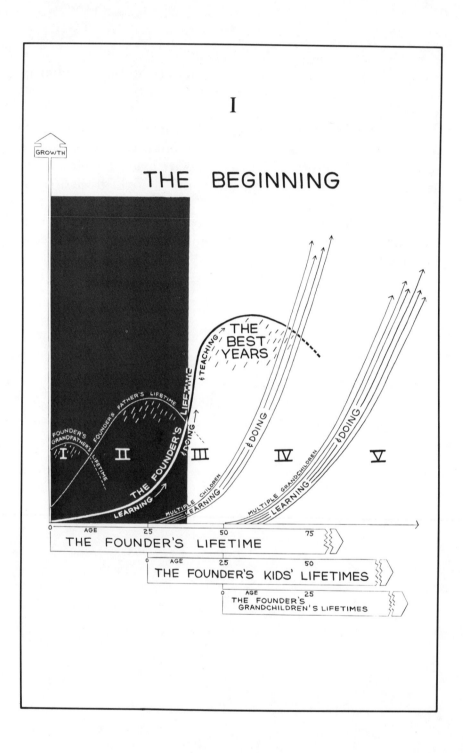

Chapter 1

Something Out of Nothing: the Entrepreneur and his Family

The definition of entrepreneur is someone with mostly nothing, because, if a man has "something," he doesn't have to become an entrepreneur. Who is this man? What's he doing in a spot like this? With whom does he surround himself? This entrepreneur is the focal point of five interlocking family generations, and he is starting an enterprise which will change the course of that family forever .

Men who found businesses are the green berets in our army of economic men. They fight their battles over all kinds of terrain--in basement foxholes, out of the garage, or the back of a truck.

They're not headquarters types. They don't work out of operations manuals--and they couldn't if they tried. Most of their time is spent struggling to stay alive against overwhelming odds. What they learn, they don't learn through training or in school. They learn by surviving. If it works, they figure, use it again.

These men learn things during their years of struggle starting a new business that the most skilled and educated management consultants could never understand. Entrepreneurs swim in white water rapids with the full knowledge that there's nobody around who's going to throw them lines or scraps of wood, or even a few words of encouragement. Mostly, what comments they do get come from critics, hecklers, and unbelievers.

They keep afloat thanks to guts, tenacity, and a vast misunderstanding about just how big the risks really are. This is *survival* . It's what the world calls being ruthless, stubborn, conniving, or even unethical.

Business founders are forced to cut corners. They're constantly shaving their margins to keep their prices afloat in a competitive market. They don't make many friends, especially among their competitors. They live on the float, a financial technique that's known as "kiting checks" in the early days, but becomes "cash management" once they're successful. They factor their receivables before the products are crated for shipment. They cut so many corners that there's not a square room in the shop. Their accounting system would do credit to a call house. It's not designed to inform, it's meant to conceal.

This is the real world of the entrepreneur. It's the world you never read about in all the magazines that praise the beauties and glories of going into business for yourself. But you can bet it's a world any successful business owner would recognize in a minute--because he's been there.

A NICE GUY LIKE HIM...

Who is this guy, this "entrepreneur"? Why and how did he get himself into the mess he's in?

He asks himself the same question night after night as he stares at the ceiling telling himself over and over that he's really a hairy-chested rugged individualist, striking off on his own path, hacking out a trail never before traveled. He's a hero, the bearer of the American Dream.

And from the other side of the bed, his wife looks at him and knows that he's scared half to death.

During this time that he's bearing the blazing standard of free enterprise up the steep hill called "success," what he's mostly doing is getting knocked around, stumbling, panting, and just generally struggling to stay alive. What little he knows about "business" and "management" at this point in his career would barely fill the shoe box he keeps his records in.

He left behind his wiser, more cautious friends, who have "real" jobs...with security, a future, and a pension. They all see him as just a dreamer who never grew up. This is mostly because he won't take their advice, even when he asks for it, which is seldom.

What they don't understand is that he couldn't take their advice if he wanted to. He has more ideas going in the air than he has resources or time to handle. If he listened to 10% of the gratuitous suggestions he gets from other people, his whole enterprise would grind to a halt in confusion. While he's building his dream, the only fuel he has to run on is a mixture of unwarranted confidence and blind hope. Doubt would just dump sugar in his tank.

FREE, BROKE, AND THIRTY

The man who starts his own business is usually in his early thirties--these are the years when emotional and occupational turning points are apt to occur. Economically, he's probably broke, flat broke--few people who *have* something are damn fool enough to start their own businesses.

Many early founders get their start because they found themselves in the street. They either get fired or they pop out of the wrong hole in somebody else's business. They start their businesses either because they "gotta," because they're "gonna show 'em," or both.

There are, of course, a small number who *did* have something--a house in the suburbs, kids in private schools, a career that appeared promising. Usually, this is more common in high technology industries. But the road they have is just as hard. In these cases, they became entrepreneurs, not because they had to, but because they *wanted* to.

Their new world changes them, though. Oh, they still go to the parties, and all the right places, and they know how to talk about all the socially interesting things, but sooner or later, the economic facts of the entrepreneur's life show up. Slowly, or quickly--depending on the circumstances--these reformed "professionals" throw aside their gentility. Very few of them make it to success holding onto their old corporate manners.

In some senses, we could say that it takes more guts to start a business when you don't have to than when you do, and it can have even greater deleterious effects. As many marriage statistics will show, the strains begin to appear as wives resent the change from what things could have been if only their husbands hadn't had their wild idea.

WHY ARE THEY WINNERS?

Still, the important question remains--why do certain people found and succeed in their own businesses? We can all make guesses, and psychologists have expended all sorts of time and money in trying to determine why. But I have my doubts whether any of them can really come up with a universal answer.

Statisticians have all kinds of explanations why new businesses fail in the first few years. The reasons most commonly given are bad management, lack of capital, inadequate experience, or some variation on those themes. However I suspect that these theories are really rationalizations of why unpleasant things happened to nice people doing the wrong things for the wrong reasons.

It's widely known that most business founders fail after the first few years. The world is filled with them. They're the losers. They just disappear. They go back to the factory, or back out on the road. They go back to the office or the drafting board. The specific reasons why they fail are really a matter for guesswork, because there's yet to be a survey that talks to enough non-bitter, objective losers to come up with a believable evaluation of entrepreneurial failure.

But what about the founders who do succeed? Don't ask them. Sober, most of them have no firm idea why they succeeded either. You can interview a great number of successful founders. You can ask them about their early training. You can play all sorts of psychological tricks with their egos, their psyches, and their answers. Many authors have done this, but I don't have a lot of faith in their results.

I've met thousands of business owners during my career, and many of them have become my close personal friends. I've slept in their houses, eaten their food, drunk their whiskey, talked with their wives, played with their kids, and struggled with their problems. I've done this for over twenty years. And after all that time, how some of them became successful still amazes me. I've got thousands of great war stories and no universal answers.

I'd almost say that the conception and raising of a successful business is a semi-miraculous event. The only thing that justifies all the hopes the founder had in the beginning is the success he achieves. Probably nobody would have been able to predict his success looking at it all from the beginning.

Old entrepreneurs and money are easily parted by the simple act of telling them "Of course you can do it again." I've seen too many successful business founders, free of the responsibility of management because they "sold out," who take their money and say to themselves, "I did it once. I know the secret. I can do it again." Mostly they fail--taking with them much (sometimes all) of the money they accumulated the first time, plus the cash, credit and reputation of those who believed in them. It's sad to watch, but you can't tell them.

What this indicates to me is that success is a combination of timing, relevance, luck, and opportunity, coming together at just the right time, with just the right amount of energy, guts, and resources. This means, any given successful founder's activities just may not be duplicable--all the more reason why their creations must not be allowed to disappear.

FOUNDERS ARE A VERY MIXED BREED

The variety of people who found and run successful businesses is simply astounding.

Some of them began life unlettered, untutored, and poor, learning what they know under difficult economic conditions, in non-establishment environments.

I'll never forget the 70-year-old founder of one of the sweetest, most profitable businesses I've ever seen, a man I met one day on a flight from Cleveland to Los Angeles. He came to the United States from the old country in his early teens. His education was minimal. His speech still bore a heavy accent.

He told me about his business and his family, and the more

he told me, the more impressed I became. Finally, I asked him what it was he thought made it all so successful. He told me he didn't know, really, that he had simply made it his goal to get something out the door every day. And that's what he did. What he, and his successors, got *done* today brings that family more than $30 million in annual sales--with a very profitable track record and a bright future.

But I've also met men from the so called privileged side of the tracks, founders who had enough degrees to paper a wall, or who had outstanding technical expertise, or who had wide experience in corporate business and professional management.

Some of these people began their businesses with a saleable product or invention or idea, and chose to leave the establishment environment they knew to strike off on their own. These people, with little experience as street fighters, pulled out of comfortable major corporations or academia, learned to scrap with the best of them, and won in a world with very different rules.

Nobody can say for sure what attributes are needed by the successful entrepreneur, but I seriously doubt, whatever these attributes are, that they are inbred. I don't believe successful business founders are born that way. They would seem to have been raised under circumstances that made them that way--from a number of different perspectives.

Not many successful founders would agree with me. Success tends to make believers out of all of us--believers in ourselves and disbelievers in luck, good fortune, and blind chance. As one business owner of long acquaintance once said to me, "I'm sure that the day the doc patted my butt, I wanted to improve his technique."

Probably. But genes don't the whole entrepreneur make.

THE GATHERING STORM

Any successful business owner, who honestly reflects on his past, will admit that his attitudes and resources, the ones that carried him through his 25-35 doing years, were picked up in his first quarter century--his learning years.

By the time he's 25, the business founder has learned his values from his parents, his technical knowledge from his education and experience--whatever it was--and picked up his circle of friends from his environment. He's also picked a mate with some degree of certainty.

He comes into his entrepreneurship armed with his own powers and limitations--physical, intellectual, and economic. Out of this backdrop, he begins to build his business, usually making a continuing series of hasty, ill-advised, or downright bad decisions based more on reaction to personal immediate needs or immediate desires, than on any careful thought about the future.

The founder chooses his business associates out of the limited group of people he knows. He puts a relative into sales because it sounded like a good idea after a few beers around the kitchen table. He picks his partners because he needs someone to keep the books straight or contribute cash--he could only borrow so much, so he had to give equity. He gathers his employees through desperation or fantasy--the only ways he can cajole anyone to join a struggling, marginal business. He spent more time, talked to more people, and accepted more ideas while picking out a name for his business then he did in budgeting his funds for the first year's activities.

This is why the business founder's background is so important to the future success of his business. It's accidental, to a great extent, whether or not he picks the right people or has the right talents and experiences to take his idea, his dream, and make it into an enterprise with a life of its own.

FAILURE IS NOT ALWAYS INCOMPETENCE

This is the reason why so many early failures are as much a matter of bad luck--bad choices, more specifically--as they are of capital and management problems. If you reach out and grab the first bodies that happen to be drifting by where you happen to be, you're playing against some massive odds in hoping you'll get the kind of help you'll need.

Add to this recruitment roulette the fact that most founders haven't the slightest idea what kinds of skills they are going to need in the people they bring into the company, and you wind up with a very explosive personnel policy.

Yet every day, I see *successful* owner-managers who made all these mistakes and succeeded. Their businesses are growing and successful, even though the brother-in-law turned out to be a lush; the partners only work half days, and really would rather be doing something else; and the old-time employees, having long since failed to produce anything significant, are cluttering up the organization like chewed bones.

The kinds of messes I find while walking through successful businesses, the clutters of mistakes that wind up giving the successful business founder migraines, constantly impress me with the staying power the individual entrepreneur has. This poor guy just has to have prodigious talent to outweigh the thousands of things he screws up. He does almost everything wrong, mostly because he doesn't know any better--but he works so damn hard, it works out.

Genius, especially in the case of the entrepreneur, is 90% sweat, applied to circumstances which are probably (if the facts were admitted) also 90% dumb luck or accident.

The successful business founder has to have an absolute singleness of purpose, almost a tunnel vision, to survive the early days. He sure doesn't get much effective help from anybody else. Years later, after a couple of martinis, this singleness of purpose becomes translated into "raw courage" or "guts" or "vision," but the reality is that the business founder doesn't usually have the time to think about what actually can happen or is happening to him.

Like most heroes, he sees something that needs doing and so he does it. It's only later that he takes the time to think about what he did. That's when his knees start shaking. Just about the time that he gets smart enough to get scared, it's too late to turn around. So he makes it. The laurels come, and, naturally, he knew it would work out all along. It's true, he *did* think it would work out, but only because he was too naive to see what he was really getting into.

This little heroic fantasy would be harmless enough if it didn't encourage the founder to become impressed with his own experience. He did it, and that means what he did was right. His managers eventually can't get through to him. His advisors have given up trying--they settle for their retainers. His successors are told to "learn to do it the way I did," presumably because whatever he did worked. I've often wondered if 30 years experience--his or mine or any one else's--is really 30 years worth, or is it 10 years repeated 3 times, or 3 years repeated 10 times? It does make you think.

Our wives, meanwhile, have to adjust to living with a god.

THE HARD ROLE FOR "MOMMA"

While Dad was plowing through the early years thinking about little other than the particular brushfire he was stamping out at any given moment, you can bet Momma has plenty of time to think about a lot of things. She has to watch from the sidelines as he drains the bank account, mortgages the house, and borrows on the insurance so he can throw it all into something she really doesn't understand. She doesn't feel proud of her hero so much as she feels generally *terrified* .

The entrepreneur needs talents and guts to survive. That's sure. But he also needs an understanding spouse. Without that, he would probably be fatally beaned by the bricks and bottles of the early days. Without that understanding, he probably would have thrown in the towel.

The business founder needs much more than his wife's understanding, although that is essential (and usually only one way--from her to him). He needs much more than her active participation, too, although she often works alongside of him and gets dirty and tired with him.

The help he really needs is to have someone to talk to, someone with whom he can share his worries, his doubts and his risks; someone who can appreciate his victories and understand the nature of his coming battles. But the entrepreneur is usually the world's best example of a rugged individualist...and that means he's tough. The idea of sharing with her his doubts and worries appears as weakness, so he won't.

His spouse is his greatest potential ally, and yet too often he cuts her out of his dreams and his pain. She may work alongside of him or she may not, but seldom does he share his burdens with her. She's alone, physically and often emotionally, as he works his 14-16 hour, 7-day weeks. The pressure on her is intense and the appreciation almost non-existent.

Even the IRS refuses to accept her help as an important component of business survival. I have on my desk a letter from an owner-manager asking if I had any idea how he could substantiate his wife's salary. She is a substantial owner of three small companies and contributed to their overall operation since their very inception without pay or reward until recently. And now she is starting to take a salary from them. The IRS wants to disallow them as "unsupported" because her existence was undocumented until the business succeeded.

I know the position taken by the tax people. It's often based on bias, misunderstanding, misinformation, and ignorance. But it's essentially the same position taken by too many business founders. Wives are too often taken for granted, expected to understand and not to complain. Only rarely are they taken into confidence to the extent they should be and, consequently, seldom do they add their full potential to the problms of the growing business.

It is my firm belief--and it's a belief based on long experience--that one of the most misunderstood and unappreciated assets in any family-owned business is the wife of the owner-manager. If a business--and a marriage--survive the early period, I wouldn't hesitate to say that it is probably as much due to an active, understanding spouse as it is to the struggling genius with his tunnel vision.

THE PARTNER IN ABSENTIA

This person, this entrepreneur's spouse, is married to an absentee. While he's off fighting the wars, winning and losing battles he never talks about, she is raising a family. It's his family, too, but as far as he sees, the kids are small, undemanding, inexpensive, and underfoot.

This kind of life isn't written into any marriage contract I've ever seen. It's surely not what the founder's wife dreamed about when she pictured marriage while she was growing up. But it's what she gets.

What she gets is loneliness, responsibility, and taken for granted. It's not that he doesn't love her--she doesn't question that either, if she understands--it's just that he's given birth to a baby of his own, his business, and that baby needs him all the time. But that realization doesn't make the founder's spouse feel any better.

She may be willing to bear the responsibility of the family. She sees that as her contribution. What hurts most is that she's unable to help her husband other than to act as a sounding board for his great ideas, an audience for his victories, and a repository for his complaints. His dreams, his frustrations, his defeats, and his fears he keeps to himself because he doesn't want to burden her.

She's not insensitive. When he comes home late every

night and eats his warmed-over supper in almost total silence, when he tosses in his sleep, snaps at the kids, looks more and more haggard, she has enough indication that something less than good is going on. He says he doesn't want to worry her with "his" problems. He's convinced that he has to solve these problems himself because he's the one who got them into the mess in the first place. He thinks he's doing her a favor.

But his wife knows. She's not blind to him and his needs. She's just helpless because he won't share with her. So the founder's wife begins to use the only thing she has left, her imagination. And, believe me, what she imagines is going on is far worse than anything that could be happening. She goes through her days with a gnawing fear of impending disaster.

This is so much different from what *he* is going through. *He* has some idea where he's going. *He* believes that he can do it. The little positive signs that crop up every day, the minor victories, register with him just as well as do the setbacks. He lives it and he believes it. But the little things are just too complex to explain to his wife. Someday, he tells himself, he'll bring her up to date.

But the years go by, while he never really fills her in. The business gets more and more complex, and, therefore, more difficult to explain to her. "She just wouldn't understand." It becomes a self-fulfilling prophecy.

Of course, it would be best if she could get him to talk. If she could demand that he tell her what he's thinking, she could maybe keep up, she could maybe help because she could know what was happening. But to force him to open up, she knows she would have to hurt him. When she sees him, he's tired, drained, and scared. Making him talk about it isn't going to do much in the short run to make him feel better. It's so much easier to let it go. It seems so much more kind.

And, thus, the first set of bricks is mortared into the founder's wall of secrecy.

WHAT SHOULD SPOUSES UNDERSTAND?

Some women don't want to know at all what their husbands do. They just want to be completely divorced from the whole thing, often considering the business to be essentially evil and a competitor. It is these women who consider the business to be their husband's mistress. They resent her and never fail to make their resentment known.

Others who are more wise than this, might accept the business as the child of their husband, but it remains a child whom they have not brought up together.

Some women are part of the business in a fictional way, under some meaningless title like treasurer, secretary, vice president, vice chairman, or some other euphemism designed to confuse the IRS into thinking her contribution has some substance.

Others are truly involved, in some cases, being more contributory to the success of the business than their husbands. She may, for example, be the inside administrator, while her husband is out massaging machinery in the shop, doing what he knows best.

Because wives fall into distinct categories, so does the knowledge they might have, or require about the business. The guiding consideration, in my opinion, is that she understand enough about the business so that she can face the future with faith rather than fear of disaster from the unexpected death or disability of her husband. She must know, accept and understand the company's managers and advisors. She must know and accept the outside directors if they exist, and she must know that they all know her and her priorities.

If the wife of a business owner is afraid of what would happen to her and her family if her husband were to leave the scene, if she is not sure what she would or should do, she does not know enough about the business. Whether her plans are to run the business herself or to leave that to someone whom she trusts, this basic criterion still applies. This state of affairs must be rectified--and the earlier, the better.

The time to begin preparing her is the time we are discussing--the early days of the business. The same applies to the kids.

THE ORPHANED KIDS

It never occurs to the business owner's kids that he needs help and support. They never see him as anything other than the hairy-chested mesomorph who has everybody under his thumb. He's strong, tough, demanding. He's the boss. He can't be bothered. He's too tired or too busy or just plain never around.

The kids grow up with Mom and what picture they get of Dad comes mostly from her. The image *he* gives them is one of an absentee relative who drops into their lives on his way to or from elsewhere. When he is around, he either makes them feel inadequate, ungrateful, or guilty. I often wonder how many of the sports cars on the road are actually guilt offerings from Dads to their neglected kids.

These kids are the next generation. They will be running the world in which we die. With luck, they will be their fathers' successors. But surely they get less attention than the new employees coming into the shop. Dads like to assume that because they have fathered their children, those children will have their fathers' values. A Dad thinks he can explain things to his kids the way he does to his own contemporaries. He's wrong.

It comes as a sad realization to those of us who are parents that our values and standards are not necessarily either known or accepted by any of the young, particularly among our own. In actuality, they've probably had the disadvantages of an absentee father, so probably very little of our value system "takes" with them. What they have seen, often, is specifically rejected. Often, what we regret in the entire new generation, we see specifically in our own children.

HE JUST DOESN'T HAVE THE TIME

It's not that the founder wants things this way. He just doesn't have time in the beginning. "Tomorrow" or "someday" things will settle down and then he'll have more time to spend with those for whom he believes he's doing it all. Despite outward appearances, the business founder is not building his dream just so he can live high on the hog.

His sole goal is not just to squirrel the money away and then retire early. His dream is to be someone, to be able to point to something he built, and to say "I did it," to be remembered with love by those who follow. He's not working just to get something. He's also working because he *loves* his work. But this simple dream gets him into all kinds of trouble in the end, because he doesn't take the time to stop and think about what it is that he's doing--and why.

Over and over again, I meet successful business founders, men who are at the height of their dream, who are confused and frustrated because things just didn't work out the way they planned.

I remember one man in particular. When I met him, he was 73 and still the president and chief executive officer of the company he founded. He'd built a beautiful organization, manufacturing an ingenius product line that had an almost infinite number of uses. His company controlled major sources of the raw materials, his cost of goods was low, his margin high. The product was excellent and had established a national reputation.

He asked me to come and help because he didn't think his sons were ready to take charge. He wanted to retire, but didn't think the 20 years two of his boys had spent in the company had prepared either one for the presidency.

I talked to his three sons. I talked to their wives and their mother. I spoke with the key managers in the company. Sadly, it soon became clear to me that the founder's only option was the sale of his business. It was too late.

The oldest son, who got a degree in engineering with the idea that he'd succeed his dad, was totally unable to communicate with the founder or advance his own ideas in the face of his father's disapproval. His father had always been a towering figure in his life, someone who awed him, but whom he never really knew or understood. Now, at 43, his spirit had left him, and he just did what he was told. He had stayed in the shadow of his aggressive father too long.

And this man, at 43, also had children who were now in their late teens and had been observing this emasculation of their father by their grandfather. Little wonder that their desires to join such an enterprise were minimal or non-existent. There is no question in my mind that the attitudes of grandfathers strongly influence the attitudes of their grandchildren, for good or for bad.

CASH WON'T ABSOLVE ABSENCE

The second son, who was 36 when I met him, had spent the majority of his time racing his expensive cars all around the world. His title was "Advertising Manager," but the majority of the advertising he produced appeared on the doors and hoods of his turbo-charged racing machines. This was the "indulged" kid. He had the misfortune of being born after the company's cash flow had finally been positive for a few years in a row.

His older brother was the unfortunate product of the founder's "blunder" period, the early days of the business when Dad only had time to be little more than the absent authority figure. He had destroyed himself trying to measure up to the impossible image of a man he didn't understand.

An earlier book of mine, *BEYOND SURVIVAL* , (Center for Family Business, University Press, Inc., 1975) defined four stages in a founder's business life cycle. Most often, the new business owner goes from the *Wonder* stage, when he wonders what in hell he's supposed to do, through a *Blunder* stage where his hard work makes up for his mistakes. This is the stage I refer to here. Following *Blunder* is usually *Thunder* , the time of the increasingly successful, and sometimes obnoxiously successful business owner. The fourth and final stage has two labels-- Plunder or *Rebirth of Wonder*--depending on how well the founder plans for the future.

But the middle son came along at about the time that Dad discovered that he had money, money he could use to give things to his kids that he never had. The younger boy became accustomed to gifts and privilege in the place of love and discipline. For him, the business was a gold mine with a bottomless vein. Depletion of resources, for him, was a way of life. At 36, with two divorces and three children from 15 to 10 living with his ex-wives, his "swinging" lifestyle was the despair of his still hard-working father.

The third son, (at 34 the brightest of the three in his father's judgment), had never been willing to work under the conditions imposed upon him by his father. He had long since carved out a career for himself and had no interest now in joining--only in getting his share of its value as his right.

The founder's wife, at 67, was a wonderful, sensitive woman. She had stood behind her husband for nearly a half-century, raising their children as best she could, year after year giving a little more of her husband up to the business. Now, she told me, they really had little in common. They still loved each other I suppose, but they spent most of their time apart. She followed her volunteer activities, and he worked, as usual. When they were together, she said, they just didn't have much to talk about. His wall was too high and too thick--and she'd grown used to it.

This man was alone at the end of his life, having accomplished everything he thought he'd worked for. He'd failed because his dream had been cluttered up by his success.

THE QUALITIES OF A WINNER

With success, the problems and concerns become too wide-ranging and subtle for talent and hard work alone. There are many bright people around with lots of drive, but they don't all build successful businesses. And here, by successful, I mean businesses that are growing, viable, and capable of being passed on to subsequent generations. To be that successful, the entrepreneur needs additional qualities over and above the common characteristics which carry him blundering through the beginning.

I haven't discovered these qualities through any formal survey. They are conclusions I have drawn from the many owner-managers I've met at various stages in their business life-cycle. Success, as I see it, is not a matter of growth or size or return on net worth. It's not even net worth. The founder's true success, in my opinion, is in the continuity of his business, and in the opportunities he can leave to his heirs.

To find this kind of success, the entrepreneur needs to develop three important qualities:

I. **He must be an articulate person with a long-range point of view.** The earliest dreams, in general, are the dreams of young men who have mostly nothing. We don't see many Princeton grads becoming entrepreneurs. They don't have to.

The new entrepreneur is a lot like a kid playing football on the street. With no alternative, he has to play there. Most budding entrepreneurs are desperate, with limited friends, cheap advisors, doubtful management, and no organization whatsoever. Their capital comes from other people and a lot of dubious dealings. (Bankers have many names for sources of capital, most of them technical and not particularly descriptive. Capital brought in from the outside is Other People's Money--OPM--and that's what I will be calling it.) Entrepreneurs are short-term thinkers with immediate needs, and they play with a gut survival instinct.

This isn't all bad. Without these attitudes in the beginning, the entrepreneur probably wouldn't make it. But once he makes it, the business begins to expand and grow. Its needs become more sophisticated and his gut instincts need to be translated into more sophisticated, longer-range outlooks. He must evolve into a professional quarterback, working out the strategies and actions that will be *needed farther into the game, and communicating them to others on the team.*

The successful entrepreneur has to begin thinking farther and farther into the future--and not just about finance, markets, and products. He must begin to extrapolate on his present "world" and plan for what it will become.

At 35 or 40, he only has 300-400 working months left to him, much less than the infinite span of time he assumes. How will he spend those months? What will he do when he stops running the business and passes it on to his successors?

His children will be approximately his current age in 25 years from now. Where will they be? What will they be doing? What will their goals be?

What do they know? What do they understand? Who is setting their value standards? What do they know about him, their father? What do they think of each other, their brothers and sisters, their cousins? What do his partners' wives think of each other as business sisters-in-law? What have they told their children about each other?

The children of business owners--and their spouses, as they arrive--tend to be isolated from the problems facing their fathers and mothers, because of the overwhelming preoccupation of the parents with the needs of their *business* child. It's hard enough for a grown man and woman to cope with change and success, but what about the kids who have little source of balance at all except from their parents?

WE MUST PRESUME SUCCESS

The founder must presume success from the outset. He must also presume that, at some point, his direct influence will end. Instead, the whole subject of retirement usually comes as a shock to this man and his wife, usually right about the time he comes to face up to it. That's usually too late. At 35 or 40, the concept of retirement seems like a fabulous idea. Golf, leisure, travel, no more sweating, grunting, cowtowing--a real, live nirvana. Let's think about doing it at 50 or maybe 55.

But why is it that when we get to be 55, retirement no longer seems all that great. In fact, it's a terrible thing to contemplate because the only alternatives seem to be 1) to die young and let somebody else solve the problems we didn't have the guts to face, or 2) to never get old and keep telling our kids to be patient.

Successful business owners must assume that someday they will be materially successful beyond their wildest notions. The questions must be asked: what will that success require of them, of their friends, of their family? What does it mean to be raising rich kids? There are so few models available to pattern our lives after.

The business founder's advisors may have been adequate in the beginning, but will they measure up to his needs in the future? By what standards are they to be judged? Is it loyalty? Or should it be competence and commitment? And who should be their judge? Doesn't the business owner have the right to be assured of their continued concern and commitment?

It's unfortunately so easy to be comfortable, and say, "You know what I mean" to people who never did understand. Our apathy can keep our business in the hands of incompetent advisors too long. It's not their fault. It's our fault. Somehow it seems acceptable for entrepreneurs to change and upgrade their neighborhoods, their vacations, and their whiskey. But somehow it never occurs to them that they might change and upgrade their advisors upon whom far more depends.

Can it be that the business owner, for all his chest beating and heroic self-image, is at heart shy, and doesn't feel he's either qualified to listen to or use the best help available? Could it be that he thinks they would laugh at him and his problems? Is he ashamed of what he thinks he's doing wrong and afraid that if anybody knew about it, his image would be destroyed?

The business owner, if he's going to succeed, will eventually have to lift his nose off the grindstone. It must happen. He can wait until it's too late, as too many do, or he can adjust his vision *now*, and begin to think about the decisions and choices which must be made today if the tomorrow of his hopes is to come to pass.

II. **The successful founder is able to redefine what requires his attention as the business grows.** Men who start businesses, but fail to change their roles as the requirements change, are the ones who become the losers.

Entrepreneurs start their businesses as extensions of the experiences they've had and the people they've met during the first 25 or so years of life. These early businesses are generally inhabited by people with whom the founder has personal relationsips. His choice of business associates is highly personal. If he doesn't have a college education, it's likely that his associates won't have either. If he has a strong ethnic background, his associates will probably also have strong ethnic backgrounds. And so forth. His past is prologue to his present environment.

Any counsellor or advisor to the business owner should always ask him how he got where he is. His responses will be true, but they'll be true the way war stories usually are. Just like the the veterans of most wars, business owners have a firm recollection today of things that mostly didn't happen. But these images that they have created over time are so vivid that they must be dealt with almost as if they were fact.

This is why children don't often listen to Dad's war stories. They also don't listen to the mistakes he made, the things he did, how he got to this point. *An intelligent aggressive listener is one of the business owner's greatest needs.* He needs someone who doesn't take sides, who asks "and then what?" and who allows him to dwell on those parts he feels are important.

It is only in the presence of a competent, contributory listener who *understands* and who *believes* in him that the business owner feels comfortable about delegating decisions that he used to make. The speaker without an audience is a person who cries alone in the wilderness.

And alone in the wilderness is usually where we find the business owner. This is why it's so frustrating trying to discuss the problems of delegation with him. He understands intellectually that with increasing complexity, there are less and less things that he can give his attention to. But, unfortunately, most of the managers with whom he has surrounded himself seem not to have the same concern for the needs of the business. In fact, they keep asking *him* for decisions in areas for which *they* should be responsible. Some employees become very adept at "delegating upwards" as a cover for their incompetence. The reason it works so well is that it reassures the boss of his indispensibility.

Just at the time when a well-oriented entrepreneur, confident of his success in the future, should start making formal plans for his organization, the business owner falls back on those techniques and interests and activities which made him successful in the beginning, even though their relevance is questionable.

Unfortunately, when he's in his forties, the business owner's organization chart is a shambles. It could be like a rake with the Ayatollah on the top and the hostages on the bottom, with the kids - militant or otherwise - scattered somewhere in between, or it could be like a big spider web, with everybody forced to make a pilgrimage to the center to see the guru, kids included. The relationships among the protagonists are either vague, antagonistic, or favor seeking.

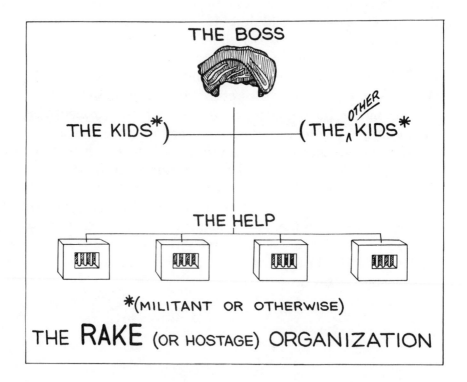

THE BOSS

THE KIDS*) — — (THE *OTHER* KIDS*

THE HELP

*(MILITANT OR OTHERWISE)

THE **RAKE** (OR HOSTAGE) ORGANIZATION

The design of a well-conceived forward looking organization chart with all of the people in it and updated, would probably be one of the best uses of a business owner's time in those early years as he looks forward to the future with hope.

This is the time to look at all his people objectively and with an eye to the future--not for their contribution to the present--because if they don't learn and grow as the business owner must learn and grow, they will just get older. This will be the legacy (or maybe the anchor) that the business owner leaves to his kids and his widow. This is why organization charts should be updated whenever changes are made, people come or go, or new organizational elements are added.

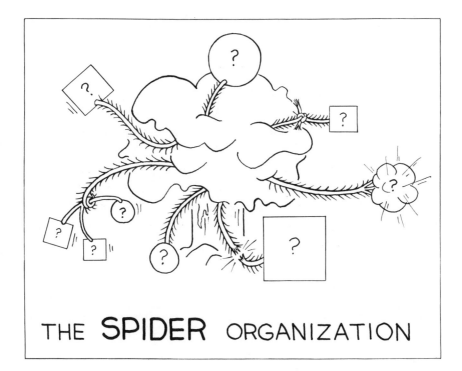

THE **SPIDER** ORGANIZATION

If the business owner won't face up to the *constant* education and upgrading of his managers, as well as the limitation or termination of those who won't improve, he will leave his successors with hangers on, who substitute tenure for talent.

The marketplace, the technology, and the environment of the future are scary enough for future planning, but there's little excuse for the business owner to add to them the shambles of managerial illiteracy and family hostility.

It's in this intellectual and economic backwater that the entrepreneur faces the challenges of change and growth. The faster he goes, the bigger the business gets, the more he is required to look farther ahead. Those who fail to make this adjustment tend to miss the important curves.

He has to break out of his backwater, to demand competence from his people, over and above the loyalty he's come to expect. He must look carefully at himself to find his strengths and weaknesses--and then begin to apply his available time and energy to the use of his abilities, not to compensating for the inadequacies of those around him.

He must realize, too, that his family needs attention, more so as they and the business grow. As much as the business needs his time and his attention, his family needs his presence, his advice, and his understanding more. They are his real investment, his real security, his real hope for the future.

III. **The successful founder and his family must be able to accept a rapid rise in socio-economic status without being destroyed in the process** . This is probably the most subtle of the requirements for success, but one of the most important. Success carries the business owner and his family into different relationships in the community. They begin to make more money than their friends and relatives. They begin to associate with different people because of added resources and freedom, as well as because of the new and different requirements that arise from the growing business.

These are difficult times. If the founder does not handle these changes with sensitivity and understanding, he can become dominated by guilt or resentment. To succeed, the founder must be able to accept and live with the responsibility and opportunity of his increasing personal wealth and influence. And, he must be able to pass this ability on to his family so that they can expand socially without destroying existing friendships or values.

There are always people who are envious of the success

of others. These people may be our relatives, or our neighbors, they may be the teachers to our children, they may be our customers or suppliers. The business owner's success--and, remember, we are only concerned with those who have succeeded--is something that those who lack the experience can only envy or take pot shots at.

Instead of reassuring and educating his family to the responsibility and opportunity of the fruits of his labor, instead of helping them become comfortable with privilege, the business owner often promotes himself with lies. He cheats on his golf score, cheats on his income tax, and all but boasts that he cheats on his wife. He's not comfortable with his changing position. He can become a very overbearing and unlikable character--no wonder his kids avoid him and others avoid his kids.

He doesn't mean to act as he does, but he's so preoccupied with staying alive--and later showing off--that he doesn't realize that the world he's entered is a world run by the rules of others, not his. A feeling of entitlement is a poor substitute for contribution.

The growing business owner faces a problem of *emergence*, the same problem faced by emerging populations in every decade of our history--the Middle Europeans, the Irish, the Jews, the Blacks, the Hispanics--any minorities who feel that flaunting their differences or importance is going to make them acceptable. Success is very little different from any other minority characteristic--and whatever acceptance there will be, will come from within.

Every man's success is a highly individual matter. Success is based on more unique attributes and attitudes than anyone could ever count. So there are many possible answers to the question of what makes an entrepreneur, but they all boil down to some combination of drive, talent, energy, commitment, genius, guts, and an encompassing dream. These qualities are what define a winner.

Chapter 2

The New Business

Opportunity carries risk, and there are few greater risks
someone can face than starting up a business. In the
beginning, it's not really a business. It's a hope. Security
is an unknown word. The family never sees Dad. Mom
is the backbone, the hero, the production manager of the
next generation. This is the "wonder" stage. Most
start-up entrepreneurs drop out here and get a real job.
Those who don't, succeed--but they have to pay.

The new business enterprise, which nobody seemed to
need during the first 2000 years of civilized life on this planet,
now all of a sudden has just gotta be. It arises from the economic
mud with the business equivalent of a biological urge. The
founder needs to have something of his own, for life support, ego

satisfaction--any of a whole number of reasons.

In most cases, this is the only major asset the new business has: *the founder's desire that it exist.* His new business is either based on an innovation, or it's a sort of "me, too," an additional marginal unit started because everybody else is doing it--the "nth" distributor, supplier or service, or some other addition to a number of accepted going concerns.

A new business is almost always undercapitalized. The founder tries to beg, borrow, or steal the money he needs up front. He does whatever he can. He tries to live on his withholding and factor his receivables when his goods are still in process. He kites his checks, he hires people on the come and offers everybody all sorts of strange inducements.

The founder has two personalities. In the back room he's mean. From his employees, he demands compliance, pliability, flexibility, and mutual deviousness. Out front, where he meets the customer, there is nothing but smiles. The customer--the only source of noncapital income--is king. A business founder will do anything in the world to placate a customer--which explains why the entrepreneur's service is the greatest.

Drop in at a new restaurant for a good example. The owner is always there. His wife is always there. He cleans the tables. He dusts. He picks up your chair and takes your coat. He is the most polite, the most hard working, the most willing to deliver anywhere, anytime.

But *he* is all this...and nobody else. His employees just work to fill the time and get the pay. They'd work for anybody who offered them a better job--and usually they do.

A MAN ON THE EDGE

The founder is all alone. His suppliers just don't seem to want to go that extra mile for him. His employees won't put in that extra hour. Everything seems to be marginal, except him. But his time has a limit. His money is too often nonexistent. His facilities are generally awful...the roof leaks and the machines won't work. Almost by definition, he does more work than everybody else, and you can bet he's going to remember *that* in the years to come. And like war stories, those memories become increasingly heroic.

He is constantly being knocked around by a tremendous turnover in the people around him. There are a lot of reasons for this. He gets mad at people who won't go along with him. They're either not loyal or not working hard enough, so to hell with them. He changes bookkeepers, banks, employees, suppliers. He's ruthless, fighting for pure survival.

This is what makes the entrepreneur so mean. He's constantly on the edge, fully aware that if something goes wrong, the business will simply go *splutt* . He has no staying power and no depth. There are a lot of others in control of his destiny--and if they don't go along with him, the business simply won't make it. It has no resiliency--only his limitless drive. There are few chances to shrug off misfortune.

THE LEVERAGE OF OTHER PEOPLE'S DOUGH

I'm not saying this founder can't survive, but the base of his survival will be his personal and uncanny knack for using OPM (Other Peoples' Money). He may call it "success," but I won't.

The "succeeding" entrepreneur loves to work on OPM. He wants the customers to pay for the goods up front, while he pays for the supplies as late as possible. He haggles with the customers to buy the raw materials in advance or lend them to him, so then he can make the product. This kind of activity generates a tremendous "return on investment," because the founder is making money on essentially no "investment" at all.

Polite people call it "leverage."

What tends to balance this situation is the fact that most lenders aren't stupid. For reasons of their own, lending institutions would really like to assure themselves that the guy they're lending to is actually in business. The statistics on early business failure lay a lot of blame on such buzz words as "capital formation problems" or "lack of investment capital," but those are really euphemisms for lenders saying to entrepreneurs "let's see a little more of *yours* up front."

Take accounts receivable financing, for example. Let's say a new business owner goes into a bank and states he's got $50,000 in receivables so he wants a $50,000 loan. The banker, having been around, will ask to have a look at the owner's debt to equity ratio. The results are very often fatal. "You've got $8,000 invested in this and you want me to lend you $50,000. Are you out of your mind?"

This is the initial source of the antagonism between emerging entrepreneurs and bankers, an antagonism that lingers on with horrendous results. It's not some smug banker who hates businessmen and wants them to fail. It's the cautious lender who doesn't want to find that he's got 10 times as much involved as the guy he's supposed to be lending to. This puts the heaviest risk on the wrong shoulders.

Government agencies are often touted as an excellent source of capital for "small" businesses. I've even talked to legislative assistants for senators in Washington who feel that the government should guarantee loans to employees who want to buy out owners. The government tries to use money to encourage new businesses, but what it really encourages is a lot of entrepreneurs to go in over their heads in ventures that usually wouldn't stand the cold light of a real investor's scrutiny.

While it's true that there are some otherwise excellent ventures that die because of problems finding capital, there are many others who succeed in spite of it. They use another form of capital. It's called "sweat equity."

SWEAT EQUITY

The beginning entrepreneur can only operate on leverage. He doesn't have any capital and so he scrounges around, any way he can, to delay his payments. The longer he can hold onto his cash--60 days, 90 days, 120 days--the longer his "lever" becomes. With OPM in his pocket, he can stock more and more inventory, and try to turn it around faster and faster, so he can make the money on the sale and pay it back.

Businesses that are successful today started out mostly running on sweat equity. There are many names for it, depending on your point of view in relationship to the entrepreneur. People call it many things: conniving, cleverness, maneuvering, hard work, or (in polite circles) negotiating. It's all the entrepreneur has in the beginning, and I wish that this sweat equity could show up in those monthly Department of Commerce figures. There's a lot of it in a lot of businesses keeping a lot of people employed, producing a lot of product. If, as Marx said, capital is frozen labor, then sweat equity is frozen guts. And it's damn real.

The professional manager of a large public company doesn't usually understand sweat equity. He's got corporate money--real money--to play with. When you have real money coming from a relatively limitless source, then you can afford to play it by the book, to go by the rules. Managers with capital behind them can take some bruising losses now because they know they'll win in the end.

Professional managers for major corporations are long-distance runners. They can pace themselves. There's time. Their competition is running at about their same speed. They can watch him and think about strategy and track conditions and the wind and all those little things. The race was planned with the coach long before the starting gun, so there may be little to do but stick to the pace and watch for minor changes.

But the entrepreneur is in a series of 100-yard dashes for

his life. He's got so little time during and between the races that there's hardly a chance to breathe. Strategy to the business founder means getting the hell out of the starting blocks and kicking more cinders into the other guy's face than he kicks into yours. There's no grand race strategy. The entrepreneur has to be quick, clever, precise, expedient and opportunistic. That's sweat equity.

Sweat harder and faster than the other guy, and you just might win the race.

A guy with nothing but sweat equity to offer has to find someone who's willing to carry him. Any idiot can lend money--or the equivalent of money--to somebody with a triple-A rating. But it takes someone who really understands the business founder and his new business to have a good enough judgment of this man and his idea to make a sound decision whether or not he's a good risk.

SWEAT EQUITY IS INVISIBLE

This doesn't mean that the investor who rejects the entrepreneur is insensitive or unimaginative. He just can't see the sweat equity, the entrepreneur's real net worth. To see that takes time, some friendship, and a lot of effort. To sell goods to a man who has no equity, no track record--no anything--has got to take some understanding and patience.

The same thing is true on the other side, from the customer's point of view. It doesn't really take a great deal of brains to sit down and do business with people of proven integrity and proven ability because they're a known quantity. But we have to ask ourselves where innovation comes from. Where do the new sources of ideas and talent that are so necessary to that buyer's operations come from?

Buyers can, and often do, say to the entrepreneur: "Look, Fella, let's see you deliver. We'll pay you C.O.D." That takes no understanding and not much more ability. Professional managers spend a lot of time learning about the use of capital and the meaning of equity, but because they don't understand the power of sweat equity, they tend to choke off one of the major sources of creativity and new ideas in this economy.

I don't advocate solving the start-up survival problem by throwing money at it. I think we can safely leave that to the government, which is so much better at giveaways. What I'm advocating is that people who are in the position to deal with struggling new entrepreneurs develop a new kind of balance sheet, with a line for "sweat equity" as an additional part of the shareholder's equity.

The new entrepreneur could use some of this same kind of thinking too. Sweat is his real contribution to the business. It's real and it has significant, tangible value. But to him, it's not capital. It's just sweat. He has his mind fixed on dollars just like everybody else, and he convinces himself he has nothing to give to anybody. He puts *himself* in the back of the bus.

THE WELL-JUMBLED BOOKS

It's almost always the same. He never has enough money, even OPM. His checkbook and his cash draw for family needs are one and the same thing. He uses banks and checking accounts to separate out his different activities. The mortgage is in one bank, the loans on his equipment are with another. It's next to impossible for him to separate company money from his own money. He collects *his* receivables, cashes *his* checks and makes out *his* deposits. It's *his* money. He stretches out *his* payables--"It's in the mail"--learns about leverage, and tries not to make the same mistakes twice. He doesn't cheat--but he *is* creative.

The business founder's affairs are generally in such a shambles that nobody really understands them, including the founder himself. But at least he knows where things are buried in case they have to be dug up for some reason. Since the help isn't all that competent, and since *somebody* has to keep track of it all, the job usually falls on him--or Momma. And, in most cases, what both of them know about accounting can usually be concentrated in the stub of the checkbook.

Take a close look at the typical new entrepreneur's books and the chances are 9 to 1 that what you'll find is that he has six different checkbooks and four different billing forms. He brings "X" dollars home for his wife to keep the family alive with, but that "X" is very fluid and downright unsure. Sometimes, it just doesn't show up at all because the business needs it first. The founder's wife, that courageous, long-suffering woman, is then left with the task of making ends meet by finding it somewhere else. Don't tell me she doesn't take part in the building of the business. The IRS may not recognize her value, but, believe me, *she* does.

After all this, whatever is left in the till is called "owner's salary." This is a fundamental mistake made by most new business owners--they don't pay themselves a regular salary. This is one reason why business owners tend to define net profit as "my salary."

Business professionals have a euphemism for these early problems. They call them either "management inexperience" or "capital inadequacy." But they are really critical stages in the owner-manager's education in what business ownership is actually all about.

I'm reminded of an acquaintance who owns a house that was left to him by his parents. Every time he needs money, he simply refinances his house. The house is bearing it, because of the inflationary housing market, but he thinks he has some sort of infinite lode.

He's forever buying his wife all sorts of presents because she "deserves the best" and they've "worked so hard." *This* is the real nature of "management inexperience" and "capital inadequacy." At some point, inevitably, the bubble is just going to burst and he is going to go bust. He has no discipline with the spending of money.

Like my friend, the new entrepreneur isn't suffering from

"management inexperience" or "capital inadequacy." He's just going broke. If he doesn't learn the lessons of "broke," things are going to blow up in his face.

MONEY'S NOT ALWAYS THE ANSWER

Fiscal responsibility is not a matter of being tight. It's a matter of being realistic and open. But openness doesn't usually happen because, after all, it's *money* that's involved, and money is more of a secret in our society than sex. This is why you could give many business founders $100,000 in their startup days and they'd blow it. This is why sometimes the very *ease* of getting money can make the business owner sloppy. He blows the money and then he has a debt, and he's not any farther along--he's just added debt to a bad business.

Mostly, the government hasn't learned this yet. Thank goodness some banks have.

This is often one of the dangers of the government loan. The entrepreneur gets a lot of money piled up on him without having had the chance to learn the discipline of what to do with it. There are many people around who are convinced that if they just had the money, they'd know exactly what to do. When some of them do manage to get it, what they usually do is blow it away.

Contrary to all the myths, new businesses generally aren't run by people who know what they're doing. They're run by people who have something to make or sell, and they *learn* what they are doing along the way.

WHO NEEDS ADVICE?

Consultants aren't going to solve this problem for the new entrepreneur. Neither is a night school MBA or a new magazine telling them about how other people are smarter than he is.

There are points in the life cycle of the growing business

when very little makes any impact on the protagonists except the payables and the receivables. In the early days, the last thing the struggling entrepreneur needs is a lot of people around asking philosophical questions. This is one of the reasons why consultants who work with start up businesses tend to die of malnutrition. A budding entrepreneur doesn't have time for such people. They would only clutter up his tunnel vision--a tunnel vision he must have if he is going to survive the lessons of the early years.

If I could talk to the business founder at this stage in his career (which I seldom do because he's just not ready to listen), I would tell him that the best advice I could give him is to open up, to begin from the beginning to share his dreams and problems with his managers, as well as to seek and *accept* advice from competent, professional advisors. The best he can afford.

There's an important difference, however, between the philosophical questioner and the objective advisor. The former is a luxury to the new founder. The latter, however, is an absolute necessity.

THE GROWING PATTERN OF SECRECY

But generally, the new entrepreneur hardly talks to anybody, except maybe to people who share his biases. So what happens is that early in the history of the business, a pattern of secrecy and intellectual inbreeding is set, and that pattern continues, bigger and bigger, as the company grows. The way the business is shaped during the startup years all too often tends to determine its form in the future.

New businesses are like new marriages. The needs and desires which drive the participants down the aisle are powerful in the beginning, powerful enough to blind the blissful parties to the real needs they will have in the future. People who get married rarely ask themselves objectively whether this is really the person with whom they want to spend the rest of their lives.

They talk about it a lot, even say it to each other, but too often they haven't the slightest idea what they're talking about. Business formations are the same way, mostly. Business founders have almost a genius for tying the knot with lifetime associates to fill short-term needs.

At least marriage is a divine institution. Though many good marriages may start off by accident, and often for insufficient reason, God tends to protect the setup by adding a few incentives to the contract. He manages to compensate the parties involved for some of the frustrations. But God doesn't intervene in corporate marriages. Here, the protagonists have to work it out by themselves--while the incentives to do so decrease, year after year.

Remember my definition of the entrepreneur--somebody with mostly nothing. If he had something really going, he wouldn't be so apt to get involved with something as crazy as starting a business. You can't start something on nothing. The business founder knows this as well as anybody. But that's okay. He doesn't have a lot of choice. The business founder is someone who is flat broke and in debt.

To him, a lawyer is a lawyer is a lawyer. What he needs is some guy out of whom he can maneuver the most advice at the least cost. His accountant gets referred to him over a couple of beers by a lodge buddy..."There's this guy who does my taxes..." The banker is chosen because he's the manager of the branch down the block from the shop.

As if this were not enough, business founders begin also collecting employees. In the early days, wages and salaries are at best unsteady and often non-existent. Like the dream of the perpetual motion machine...people keep trying over and over again to support a payroll without any cash flow.

It's a fact that a new, struggling business just does not often attract top-notch people and employees. What it gets are more likely to be kids, drifters, relatives or in-laws. The ones who hang on are usually bribed to do so by some ill-defined promises and a lot of fast talk from the founders.

THE ACQUISITION OF PARTNERS

If the founder "needs" a partner, he hits the pavement desperate and short of breath, and begins gathering around him a whole corps of lifetime associates. Really, he doesn't need a partner so much as he needs a *backer*, but since nobody in his right mind would back such a crazy idea, he looks for a partner.

There's a vast, shadowy group of closely held business investors who fill this partner-backer role. Many of them seem to be dentists. Some are insurance agents. Some are relatives. It doesn't matter. He sees them too often as pigeons. They are people who can put up the money while the entrepreneur put up the guts and the brains--and the work.

Sometimes these "partners" aren't always silent financial backers. Often a man who is a super technician realizes he needs to have someone back at headquarters managing the help, or romancing the customers or keeping the creditors confused, making the product, or hiding the inventory from the IRS. I've seen many successful businesses in which one founder is out pounding himself silly, while the other "partner" sits back administering costs or enjoying expense account lunches. It's not that both mem aren't working, it's just that the irreplaceable input making the business grow is coming in different amounts from different partners. Sometimes, those with an equal share in the take, share little of the burden. Sometimes, the changing needs of the business requires new and different roles for the founders--and some partners won't change--or their wives won't accept it.

This is why partnerships are so often unstable. Too often, differential contribution by the partners begins to become a very sticky issue. Or each partner has a different idea of how much his heir should be involved. It may even be that both partners contribute equally, but the perception each has of the other tends to become more and more unacceptable. Or maybe their kids don't get along with their business cousins. Or maybe their wives--the business sisters--have developed a long-standing feud. Often the problem just can't be resolved and the partners, together, shoot a profitable business in the head.

Sometimes one partner can buy out the other at a price that won't cripple him and the business for too long, but buy-sell agreements aren't always good solutions because the kids of the non-survivor are often thus disinherited from a stake in their father's business.

IF I'D ONLY KNOWN...

This is the cast that's assembled to take the new little business into the future. It's assembled by an ambitious desperate man in need, in a hurry, and without any thought about how long and how close he's going to have to live with these people. I hear it over and over again: "If I'd known I was going to have to live with that S.O.B. for the past 30 years, I would never have..." There's no sex to bail these business marriages out, or even to make them tolerable.

The new entrepreneur is marginal. He's a marginal client. He's a marginal employer. He's a marginal customer and supplier. This is inevitable, because he is starting with nothing. He surrounds himself with marginal people who don't have much else better to do. This, too, is probably inevitable, but the long-term problem arises because the founder doesn't approach these early relationships like the passing affairs or casual acquaintances they should be. Instead, he gets married over and over again. He forms lifetime bonds by passing out equity to anyone who smiles at him, or by making promises and pledges he can't back out of later because he's basically a decent guy, or by simply falling into the trap of equating loyalty with contribution.

If he fails, of course, none of these mistakes really matter. In that case, everybody fades back into the woodwork and complains about the inequality of the system. But this isn't a book about the losers. It's about the winners. The business founder I'm talking about *makes it* . He succeeds. He grows. His business eventually becomes much more complex than he could have ever imagined in the beginning. What stays marginal, in general, are the advisors, the managers and the employees. He keeps them around because they stuck by him when things were tough. If the business owner is anything, he's loyal.

I'd like to be able to do a favor for every new business owner and appear to him as the ghost of his business future. I'd like to turn his clock forward 20-30-40 years to the time when he is successful, wealthy, and powerful--a pillar of his community. I'd like to show him that he will be responsible for millions of dollars in sales and tens or hundreds of jobs. His business will be a key element in the local economy. Then I'd show him surrounded by storefront professionals, inadequate managers, and substandard employees--most of them people he will recognize as cronies he picked up in the past without any thought for the future.

Someday, because he didn't think about who it was whom he was joining in bed so blithely, he will wake up to find that his business has outgrown his experience, his advisors and his management team. He will find himself working harder than he ever did in the beginning, because it will be his responsibility to struggle to make up for bad advice, incompetent management, inadequate organization, greedy relatives and his own lack of sophistication. Worst of all, he will continue to play everything close to his massive, but inadequate chest.

KEEPING THE MANAGERS "BAREFOOT"

Much of this secrecy haunting the owner-manager in later years stems from his own misunderstanding of sweat equity. Looking at a new business only from the financial point of view is a frightening experience, especially for the owner. There's no "balance" in the balance sheet, and little income in the income statement. The profit and loss statement is half misnamed. There's nothing to show the potential value of the investment of the founder's own hide. Although he believes in his own sweat equity, he probably can't define it for you, and he sure doesn't explain it well to his managers.

The founder convinces himself that if his managers are going to work, he just can't tell them too much. The more they know, the more they'll worry--and then they won't do anything. So he tells them nothin', or if they know too much, they'll want too much--so again he tells 'em nothin'.

If he would just give them a little more knowledge, a little more understanding of his planning process, or his ability to cope, if he would just give them a little more information, he would be giving them the *ability to invest some sweat of their own.* They could use *their* heads to contribute to the profit structure. If they could understand what he understands, just think of what they could do together.

But this makes it even more imperative that his managers be of the right stripe. If he can't trust a man with his capital, he should fire him. The same is true if he can't trust his managers with his *knowledge*. If a man isn't smart enough or willing enough to be taught, then the best thing, for the business *and for him* , is to help him find another teacher in another school where the personal chemistry fits better.

But owners get blackmailed sometimes by fear of the consequences. The price keeps going up--and after a few years tenure sets in. These employees get raises and promoted and then have to be dealt with later on at such tremendous emotional and financial cost--all because the boss didn't have the guts to do something about it earlier.

This problem, of course, is compounded beyond belief when blood, marriage or "friendship" are at issue in addition to incompetence.

THE FOUNDER'S WORLD

Because the entrepreneur surrounds himself so often only with the *substandard employees* he thinks he can afford, he is forced into doing most of the important work himself. If he's lucky, he will find some malleable and fiercely loyal major-domo to handle the most complex and burdensome of these secret duties. Sometimes this person is his wife. Often it's a little 52 year old maiden lady with a moustache who keeps the books. (Before I get myself in trouble with this image, let me also say it can be a 48 year old bald-headed bean counter with garters on his sleeve and a green eyeshade--take your pick--but the fact is that in reality, he/she does not *keep* the books, he/she *hides* the books. His/Her main job it to keep the help more confused than the boss.)

This is the beginning of the "rake" organization. There's the Boss on the top and all the employees lumped together way down at the bottom. Put the bookkeeper in the middle of the system and his organization chart begins to look like a series circuit with a big open switch between the power source and the load.

I've seen this kind of organization in companies with hundreds of employees, doing many millions of dollars in annual sales--and it all started years ago in the garage where the founder and his part-time help handled the first order.

As if marginal management weren't enough of a burden, because the entrepreneur so often tries to use his *advisors* on the barter system, he ends up with the kind of advisors who are willing to work for free services and/or discounted product purchases. This sets another pattern, the pattern of incompetent or inadequate professional advice.

In advisors, as in most things, you get what you pay for. I'm convinced that a large part of the mistrust of professionals by successful business owners stems from the early years when they dealt with the least qualified professionals they could find.

They've never experienced the kind of help they can get from top people, so the odds are that much increased that they never will. It's like the taste for good whisky--it's not developed by a lifetime of guzzling white lightning out of Mason jars.

Because the entrepreneur puts together his accounting system on red-eye flights and the backs of envelopes, his control systems are limited by the number of pockets he has in his suits. Because he usually knows nothing about accounting, he doesn't use it. Because he doesn't use it, he never gets to know about what a powerful help it can be to his business.

These are but a few of many "becauses." The past is prologue to the present. This is why the early years of any family business should be the most fascinating years for students of business. The entrepreneur starting his own business and struggling up the sand dune of success runs his business like a back room poker game. Hell, if anybody knew what was going on inside, they'd call the cops.

This is why most start up businesses fail. This is why it's so important that those entrepreneurs who don't fail realize what a precious thing it is that they created, and that they make plans for its continuance. Business babies like human babies are the result of love and hope, and it is fully irresponsible in my mind not to feel responsible for their transition into independence and strength in their own right.

These are the years when the business-that-is-to-be is the business-about-to-become.

Chapter 3

The Early Price of Success

The costs of success in family business are usually taken out in energy, time, health, and emotion right up front. Dad pays his price with his health, with his time, with lost time with his children, with his marriage and his recreation, with an ever-narrowing concentration on The Business. Mom pays in doing it all alone, in never seeing her husband, in watching him suffer. The children pay in missed understanding of what the business is all about. This price is paid in installments, year by year, and often the real cost is not noticed or understood until it's almost too late. It's a lot like the lily pads that cover up the lakes and double each year. Usually nobody pays any attention do them until the lake is half covered.

The business founder's success doesn't come cheaply. Just as wisdom comes with a price--age--success is only possible when its own heavy price is paid--up front. Just how that price is paid, and how much, and by whom, has a great impact on the future both of the business and the entrepreneur, but too often the new business owner doesn't realize the limitations on what he can pay.

Too often he's paid too much *unnecessarily* .

When the business founder set out on that new venture his friends called "insane," he had mainly three things going for him. He had his *talents*, which were given. He had his *resources*, which generally weren't all that much. And, finally, he had his *time* , which is limited absolutely by the rotation of the sun and the grace of a loving God. These three bits of wealth--talent, resources, and time--were the grubstake out of which he financed his new operation. He had nothing else to give.

The entrepreneur's *talents* were products of his background. They came out of his genes, they were pounded into shape by his experience, and they were expanded or eroded by the operation of choice or chance.

Talents come in different forms and in different amounts to each of us without our ever having much to say about their kind or quantity, but they remain critical ingredients of success. No successful business founder ever made it without some particular genius, some overwhelming ability that enabled him to rise above his contemporaries and his competitors, and become "The Best" at what he did.

Talent has the useful property of growing more valuable the more it is used. This makes it an almost limitless resource--as long as its limitations are understood. Unlike his other advantages, the entrepreneur's talent is generally not drained as one of the painful prices of success. What happens instead is that talent gets "leveraged"--more and more as the years go by.

Unfortunately, the business owner expands on his talent like a fish story until he gets to the point where he starts investing more than he actually has. Talent seldom gets over spent--but it often gets overblown.

THE LIMITATIONS OF TALENT

In the beginning, this was not so undesirable. After all, the poor guy needed all the confidence he could get to make it through the crossfire of the first years. A little fantasy goes a long way when we're trying to survive. But the growing business invariably demands an ever greater range of talents, and seldom is there anybody else in the business who can fill these demands. The best and hardest working employee is the owner, so he fills the gaps--or, at least, he covers them--irrespective of his talents.

Again, in the beginning this was necessary. A new business has few luxuries and the founder has little choice.

For example, I know a truck driver who started his own shipping company because he was tired of working for someone else. He knew the trucking of produce inside out, and he was the best diesel mechanic in the Northeast. The business grew. He added more trucks. Because he was aggressive, had contacts, and knew how to sell, his business grew year after year.

But because he needed every cent he took in for new equipment in those first years, he couldn't afford to hire mechanics, or accountants, or even very much office help. So who did all that? The owner, that's who. He did it all. Because it all seemed to work--he didn't go broke and the trucks kept rolling--he believed that he could do anything if he just put his mind to it. "Who needed all this expensive help and advice?" he thought, "I did it myself and look where I am."

So he started leveraging his talent. He knew sales and he understood maintenance. He did it himself so he could cut costs. Those were his talents. But instead of concentrating on them, instead of becoming the best at what he could do best, he used the earning ability of his talent to underwrite his involvement in activities he knew little more about than the people driving his rigs. He said, "if I'm good at some things, I'm good at everything.'' That, of course, means just that, everything--sales, finance, administration, personnel, government regulations...everything.

Like most unwise borrowing, this structure he's building takes some time to show signs of collapse. The results show up in his sucessful years, when he's spread so thin that he has to run over everything at last twice to make sure he's covering it. The price of "talent leveraging" is committed early, but it's exacted much later, when there's no real *management hierarchy* to handle the expanding problems, very little delegation, and even less respect for the informed opinions of others.

The first price of success is that it tends to push the entrepreneur into mortgaging his abilities up to their armpits. When he finally realizes what he's done--if he ever does--it's often too late to begin to pay off the debt.

HIS NATURAL RESOURCES

The entrepreneur's *resources* are his funds, his health, his family, his education, his experience, and his reputation. Many of these he recognizes, some of them he understands, but very few of them does he appreciate.

Probably his most obvious and appreciated resource is his *funding* . He has whatever money his personal qualities have enabled him to acquire in the past--usually some assets and some savings. In some cases, he may have access to the savings of other people, savings he can tap because of the relationship he has with them. Either they are friends, family, or an understanding banker who's willing to lend him the savings of strangers.

The business founder is always trying to expand his available funding. If he's lucky enough to have a track record, he can get more funds from the bank, but he can also get more money from his family because they're sort of cornered by blood or other ties into feeling that they should support him. Some of his funding also comes from the people who are willing to mix their labor into the common cause by becoming partners, corporate or otherwise.

He needs these capital resources because that's what he thinks he has the least of. He thinks his resource of talent is immense. He assumes he has infinite time. If he only had *money*, then he could really do it.

In the beginning, it's just a matter of staying alive. If he could only get his volume up to X bucks a year, he'll have it made. If only he could get his plant built. If only.... He gets lost in the subtle distinction between ambition and chronic dissatisfaction with his life. This is one price of his need for money.

I've seen so many *successful* business owners who have taken this basic need for money and twisted it slowly into a form of neurotic greed, usually disguised under the name of "security". All they want is just a little bit more. Their hallmark is the phrase: "If only..."

THE DRAIN ON THE BODY

In the face of limited capital funding, he depends unrealistically for money on the cash flow from a growing business, not realizing--or if told, not believing--that a growing business absorbs all the cash it generates and then some. After all, his plan is "different." So he is forced to compensate with another of his assets--his health.

The demands of the business on its owner are enormous and wide-ranging. While he's leveraging his talents and his funds to fill those demands, he usually finds he has to compensate more and more for his inadequacies by taking the last ditch contributions from his body. He stays up too late, he works too long, he worries too much, and he doesn't exercise.

Society always has its own compensations for this kind of self-abuse. It usually takes the form of short-term pleasures--rich food or booze or butts or broads, you name 'em...all short-term gratifications with long-term deleterious results. But for the founder, this self-abuse can take on the aura of a badge of courage. It can be his proof to the world that he is succeeding despite all of the odds.

The gratifications become his reward, his "just" reward. If somebody dares suggest to him that he'd better work fewer hours, drink a few less drinks, down a few less steaks, he ignores them with a martyred expression. Hecklers just don't understand. It's gotta be done. He's gotta do it. He needs the money.

Success takes its price right out of his powerful hide, while he encourages the theft. To him, that's just the way it is, because nothing happens if you don't work for it. The toll begins to show up later, in the years when he could use his health to enjoy everything that he's earned.

In the early years, while the business was being built, his wife saw him very little. When she did see him, he was burning the candle at both ends, more ready for a drink and escape into TV than to discuss and share with her what was happening. Later, when there is finally time and money to do all the things they want to do, they too often don't...because he has forgotten how or doesn't have the energy.

THE EMOTIONAL COST

There are other prices paid besides the drain on his health. From the very beginning when the entrepreneur was struggling to compensate for his capital shortage, his family was paying an emotional price.

Since most entrepreneurs started out somewhere as good employees for someone else, they appear to their relatives as bums. After all, they gave up a "perfectly good job" to get involved in some nonsense.

There's never enough money. His wife's friends always have more because *their* husbands weren't crazy enough to go into business for themselves, and somehow they always seem to succeed. The question always hangs around like a circling buzzard: why doesn't he quit and do what all these others are doing? The whole idea of the steady job takes on a fascinating glitter for this scared and dubious wife.

In most cases, this situation is something her experience never prepared her for. As far as she is concerned, she's thrown right into opening night with no rehearsals--and it's very much for real. Everything important to her is tied up in this new venture. Her marriage is at stake. Her husband works too hard, and he never sees the kids. She constantly wonders...is that her role and responsibility, to raise the kids...alone?

What her family wanted for her she sure isn't getting. She essentially rejected her family's dream in favor of her husband's, and what she got was a world that seems to be one constant earthquake. She married a plumber, or a mechanic, or a salesman, but all of a sudden he decides to change a steady job for an unsteady job. Or maybe his father had a business, and he worked for him for as long as he could take it. Then he quit, throwing up a wake of all kinds of hard feelings.

Either way, he says, "The hell with it. I won't do it. I'll start my own business." And his wife, the girl who married a nice guy, all of a sudden finds herself a *founder's wife* .

LIFE AS A FOUNDER'S WIFE

However they come to be that way, founders' wives have this stubborn tendency to have come from a past totally different from their husbands'. The likelihood that the new entrepreneur married the girl next door, bringing together families who lived together, loving and understanding each other, is less than slim--you could almost define that kind of situation as Utopia.

No, what tends to happen instead is that one is the Christian who married the Jew, the immigrant's kid who married the local catch, or the valedictorian who married the drop-out. She crosses to the wrong side of the tracks...in whatever direction.

Both families say "We had greater dreams for you," while *his* family tells her: "It's all *your* fault. He wouldn't have done all this if he had married the right girl."

Money could cure some of this, of course, but it's not available in the beginning. She didn't even want money--in the beginning. She didn't marry him because he was going to be an entrepreneur. She just married him because she fell in love with him. They love each other, and the two of them grow together and go through all the economic struggles, but tragic situations can develop. Over and over again, I've seen women who aren't accepted by their husbands' families, who are always one down. And, naturally, her family never did approve of *"him"*.

You can write your own script. Maybe her husband's brother had a steady job, and she keeps being harassed by her sister-in-law and her mother-in-law, because her husband would have been somebody if he hadn't married her.

Every founder's wife begins married life as someone's daughter-in-law, a role she can only avoid if her husband is an orphan. The world is hard enough on a daughter-in-law, but when she's also the wife of a business founder, it can be downright cruel.

These are the prices the founder's wife pays for the shortage of capital, and they are costs which don't disappear when the business becomes successful. Along with him, she starts paying the price up front.

THE MISAPPLICATION OF TIME

The entrepreneur overspends his money yes, and his health, yes, and the emotions of his family, yes, but other resources are wasted just as surely--mostly as a result of his misapplication and overassumption of his major asset, *time.*

Where the business owner puts his time is where he puts his heart, his dreams, and his thoughts. It can't be otherwise, because time steadily ticks by and every moment is just as important as the next. The minutes follow each other in relentless procession, and they can never be duplicated.

Yet the entrepreneur in his early years spends prodigiously of his time, with very little sense of priority. In doing so, he tends to waste his resources. All he gets every day is 24 hours. So to get everything done that he must get done, he steals from his sleep, he steals from his energies, he steals from his limited reservoirs, whatever he thinks he must do, in order to survive. He works 16-18 hours a day, seven days a week.

He abuses his health. He abuses his family and his friends. He doesn't have the patience, the understanding and, often, the guts to take time out from his relentless pursuit of survival. He is beset with the inevitable entrepreneurial disease called tunnel vision, the single-minded pursuit of objectives regardless of the cost to himself or to others.

He's kind to his wife, but he tends to ignore her contributions. His children sort of crop up. His employees and managers are seen as people with whom he must cope, rather than answers to problems. He sees his advisors as people he wants to get the least involved with as possible.

It never occurs to him that some time must be invested in *explaining* to others. So, the advice or assistance he gets back is the least there is in time, compassion, commitment or contribution. Small wonder he sees himself as the only person who can compensate for the inadequacies of others.

As long as the business owner doesn't understand how to use his time to gain the time and talents--and resources--of others, he will be limited to what little of those commodities he, himself, has. If he had infinite time available to him--as he seems to assume--he could carry the load himself. Instead, even the little bit he has, he tends to waste.

HE PLAYS A LOT OF ROLES

The business owner leads a four-faceted life and that means he must divide each 24-hour period into segments. He is first of all a *human being,* of course, and he must fill his physiological and psychological needs. The trouble is, in this early stage, his needs as a man can be summed up by one word: survival. All other niceties of mental and physical health are generally ignored.

Secondly, the business owner is just that, an *owner*. In the beginning, this role is insignificant everywhere except in his dreams, but it becomes more and more demanding as the business grows. Third, because his title is president and because he makes all the decisions, the business owner is a *manager*. Actually, the amount of managing he really does is miniscule, because he spends most of his waking hours concentrating on his fourth role, that of an *employee*.

Business founders spend more time than they should, as employees mostly, because they don't know what else to do. Instead of trying to figure out why their products won't sell, they just keep tampering with the product. A manager would look at how the product is being sold, or at least whether or not it has a real market. But the business owner, because of the *way* he chooses to spend his time, usually misses the jugular of what he does because he gets immersed in the detail, all the little things an employee in the fledgling empire is concerned with. He's not leading anything. He's leading only himself.

The owner-manager's available time is really both a current and fixed asset. His future and the future of the business depend upon his earning power. And that earning power is a function of his time. Every minute that he chews up is gone forever, like the oil we are pumping from underneath the deserts. Each minute that goes by depletes an irreplaceable resource. He doesn't even have the advantage of slowing production or stopping it altogether. It just runs on--and out. He's facing a shortage. It's inevitable. Yet the new business owner is forced by circumstances and his own lack of understanding to squander his most priceless resource.

The time he should be spending building for the future, he spends coping with the present. He's harassed constantly by brushfires and snipers that keep forcing him to ignore the future. He answers the phone whenever it rings and talks to whoever calls, because he's so grateful that somebody knows he exists. He opens the mail and gets all embroiled in such serious questions as the design of the letterhead, the vacation schedules of his employees in the office, or whether it's better to give a ham or a turkey to the boys in the shop for a Christmas present.

This manager, who is really an employee, does these things in the beginning because he has to. In the beginning, *he* is the guy who opens the shop every morning after picking up the mail. *He* opens the envelopes and sorts it all out on *his* desk. Then *he* makes the product and fills the orders, carrying the checks to the bank and making the deposits. It is *his* job, because *he* is all there is.

But success eventually begins to demand its price, its share of his time. The business grows. Employees are added. The accounts become more complicated and the cash deposits more involved. He's still opening the mail every morning, but now it takes him longer. Instead of the 12-hour day, he now works 14. Invoices sometimes arrive at the customers with coffee spots on them because he eats at his desk.

The need of the business for a *manager* begins to increase every day, while its demands on his time make it more and more impossible for him to think beyond next weekend.

THE PRICE OF PROBLEMS IGNORED

As it inevitably does, time passes. The business grows and the founder gets older. He's at the top of his heap, successful and well-financed. The struggles have paid off, but now he begins paying another price, the price of ignoring the problems that are piled up all around him like tank traps, limiting his options, stopping his progress.

He hasn't taken time to build a management team. Instead he just made do with whoever walked in and happened to stick around. Even the people who stayed haven't had any training because he never took time to teach them.

He hasn't taken the time to install an orthodox accounting system. What he has is a set of custom-made books that resemble a labyrinth designed by the blind. The very thought of redesigning the system he evolved with such pain reduces him to shivers. He can barely keep track of it all now. With a new system, he'd lose altogether what little control he has.

He hasn't had the time to spend with his kids, helping them understand his business and the business world. Hell, he hasn't even had time to watch them grow up. The most common thing he says when he sees them is "My, how you've grown!"

He hasn't had the time to think about succession or his retirement. That's all "later" or "someday." First things first. What he forgets is the unalterable fact that succession planning is *a process that takes years*, not the months he's going to try to do it in when it is too late. He forgets that retirement is another career, not just a sudden cessation of activity. It, too, must be prepared for very carefully if his harvest years are going to have any value at all.

But he doesn't have the time. It's all been invested in success. He doesn't even have the time to take out his interest.

Most sadly, he doesn't have the time to spend in enjoying and planning for the future with the most important person in his life, his wife. Her time is going by, too, also being invested irretrievably in their mutual success.

BOTH OF THEM PAY

Laying the groundwork for tomorrow requires some questions early in the process. The new business couple should look ahead 10-20-30 years when success has been achieved and the time left to do other things is becoming very limited. What will they have paid for what they wanted to do? What will she have given up over the years to pay the price demanded by success?

Two people starting a business bring together some very different needs. For him, security probably means being able to eat every day and having some control over his fate. For her, it's that her husband be around, that she and the kids won't be helpless and dependent should something happen to him. He takes her companionship for granted. She wonders when--and if--she'll see him again.

His source of status and meaning is his work. He is fulfilled by his success in his business. But what does she have to give her status? Is it being seen in a new Seville? Is it having her husband be the president of his own company? Is it going to the country club or having a winter tan? He gets his kicks in closing sales or opening markets. Where does she get hers? What does she need to make her time full and worth living?

The business founder is struggling day to day to achieve something that he is convinced will fulfill him. He has freedom. He is his own boss. Within the limits imposed on him by the business and the markets, his chances of reaching his dream are at least within the realm of possibility. But what about this young woman who is trying to fulfill her own dream as her own person? She is often restrained from seeking goals which are contrary to or in conflict with what her husband wants. The business is often too demanding to allow her total freedom to do what she wants. The result is that she may have to accept a modification of her dream in order to supply support, understanding, and commitment to the needs of the venture.

And he *needs* her support, understanding, and commitment. Without them he won't have the energy or even much of the ability success will demand of him. The business has to be *their* dream if the future is going to hold together. But too often another of the prices paid for success is that there is never enough time or energy left to allow them to share the concerns of the business and the opportunities of the future. All too often the dream stays *his* dream because it has nowhere else to go.

A NEW WORLD FOR WOMEN?

The social demands placed on women are constantly evolving and becoming more complex. What was once enough may no longer be, and this can cause a great deal of conflict. For many women this often means emancipation, and this they may demand from their husbands in time or equivalent. Founders, after all, aren't the only ones in need of "more."

Unlike the wife of the public corporation executive, a business owner's wife doesn't have her demands tempered by the existence of a higher authority. There's no boss to say, "Look, if your wife is going to bug you like that, why don't you just get another job?" These constraints don't exist for the wife of a business owner. Her demands that she continue to have a certain lifestyle can be so persistent and so constant, that he finally gives in to her the way he would to an insistently demanding child. For this, they both pay a price.

The wife of the business founder has to understand the price she will have to pay for success. But her husband has to understand, too, that a steady diet of black bread is as potentially destructive as overindulgence.

I remember a 66-year-old woman talking to a 35-year-old at one of our seminars. She summed up the wisdom of her years this way: "It's not a bad life, my dear", she said, "You've just got to realize that there's a price to pay. There are a lot of lonesome nights when your husband is going to be away. There's wheat and there's chaff, and in the beginning you just have to get used to eating a lot of chaff...together. That's the only way that having it later is going to mean anything."

This is why the dream has to be shared from the beginning. Both husband and wife have to understand the costs as well as the benefits of success if they are going to work toward the future together. They must be committed to sharing the good with the bad.

But I'm not advocating absolute sacrifice. Time is too precious for that. I've seen too many couples who have waited too long to enjoy the fruits of their labors, who have given up too much--both as individuals and as a family--to be able to change or put it all back together. They sowed potential and wound up reaping ashes. A business owner and his family must make sure that they take some of their precious time to enjoy themselves and whatever benefits they have available.

WE MUST CONSIDER WHAT OTHERS THINK

The entrepreneur has made his choice. He founded his business and likes what he's doing. But there are others in his life--his wife, his children, his partners and his managers. He must ask himself constantly if *they* like what *they* are doing, what is being done to them. Do they feel participative in the process of growth, or are they mostly enchained by it?

The times are definitely changing. The sharing of the dream is becoming even more critical. The concept of the dutiful, compliant wife is not what it was 10, 20 or 30 years ago. Nor is the concept of "teenager." The kids are forming some very strong ideas very early, and if they are born into a growing family business, the opinions they form about it--opinions so critically important to the continuity of the business--depend upon what is shared with them.

Their opinions are formed by what they see and what they are told and what they understand and accept. If they are told little and see only the bad things, we can be fairly certain that just about anything will look better than a career in the family business.

Sadly, it is in the early days of the business, the days when the young adult minds are being forged and formed, that the founder is off at the plant working as though there were nothing else in the world but his business. He is constantly embroiled in economic battles and the needs of his family are constantly forced farther and farther out onto the periphery. This leaves it to Mom to provide both book and music to the passion play called "family life."

The prices must be paid. The founder pays the price of missing the experience of his children. His wife pays the price of too much responsibility, self-sacrifice and solitude. The dream must be shared--if not, the children may pay the price of bitterness and misunderstanding, as they are consistently educated into the wrong impression.

Success drives a hard bargain, levying exhorbitant prices which must constantly be fought. If they are paid without thought or mutual acceptance, they just can't be afforded.

Chapter 4

Lighting the Long Fuse

Because of the struggle, the drain on time, the demands on attention levied on the founder and his family by the growing business, because of the many misjudgments and mistakes which are made in the beginning years, little booby traps are laid in the foundation of the business. They might be on a long fuse, but that fuse is not infinite. Eventually--inevitably, if they're not defused--these little bombs start going off. Somehow, these mistakes must be corrected. The future depends on it.

When the founder of a business is in his 30's--and if he succeeds at what he's doing--in 15-20 years he's going to be in his 50's and wealthy. Those are facts. He can't be sure of course he's going to succeed, but it's something he'd better plan for from the beginning, because if he doesn't, most of the problems I'm going to talk about will surely come up.

The founder may have a kind of mystical "sense" that he will succeed--that he's destined for great things--but he seldom has the slightest idea what success will really mean. Instead he has a blind faith that all his problems would be solved if he could only have 10% more volume, 10% more productivity, and 10% less harassment. He believes the solutions to his problems are just around the corner.

Every act has consequences for the future--some known, some unknown, some predictable, some unpredictable. Tomorrow's facts are usually formed in today's acts--acts either committed or omitted, conscious or unconscious.

One thing is sure. There *will* be consequences of our acts--of going into business with a given partner; exchanging or giving up equity for capital; hiring and firing of personnel; choosing, accepting, and rejecting of opportunities. The consequences may take time to show up--but they will. The new business is minimal, so the effects of decisions are minimal in the beginning. But *tomorrow*, when the business is no longer marginal, their impact--for good or bad--will be great.

The fuses of an explosive future are unknowingly lighted by the entrepreneur. Because of his nature, as well as the nature of his business, he makes certain choices, takes certain paths, all with long-range consequences he fails to foresee. He just *does* things, in such quantities that he's able to ride the crest of a vast number of mistakes to the solid ground of success. But the "sweetness" of what success he eventually achieves depends on the course he steered, the people he brought with him, their abilities, and attitudes--and his.

All of his choices carry consequences for the future. Some carry more. Some carry less. Usually, when I finally meet this entrepreneur, he is sitting precariously on all kinds of sensitive explosives which he planted year by year as the business grew.

What he tells *me* is that things just haven't worked out the way he planned. What I have to tell *him* is that things didn't work out precisely because he didn't "plan" at all. He knew not what he was doing.

THE PRICE OF SECRECY

One of the first mistakes the owner-manager makes when setting up his management "system" is to draw the blinds. He's afraid if the employees find out how bad things are, they'll quit. So he keeps the figures to himself and covers up the problems. Unfortunately, success doesn't cure his bad habit. If anything, it makes it worse.

As the founder succeeds, he begins to make money. Because he owns the business and is the main source of its earning power, he keeps more of that money than anybody else. But this leaves him with some strong feelings of "impropriety." He feels that somehow his earnings out of the business will be misconstrued by the help. He worries that if they know what he takes out, they'll get all upset. So he continues to hide the figures.

In our society it's easier to talk about sex than it is to discuss money. Money is like the "Yahweh" the biblical Jews could never utter, under pain of death.

It's not unusual for the new owner-manager, for example, to open the mail and do the deposits himself to keep everyone from learning how much he's making. He can't do this for long, of course. The growing business just gets too complex for that. But the idea is maintained through his accounting system, his chain of command (which is little more than a chain of obedience), and his ever-growing habit of secrecy. If you ask many a new business owner what time it is, he'll ask you why you want to know.

It never occurs to him that if he just went ahead and *gave* people the information they need and let them do the work, he'd get a lot more work *done* and at lower overall cost. Beyond the morale and efficiency issues, there is the question of effectiveness. Managers who are denied accounting information can't really be creative or flexible. Accounting data is both the measure of their performance and the determinant of their actions.

What happens instead is the boss hides the books and the managers have to operate in ignorance and confusion. The vicious cycle begins: the boss assumes the managers are inadequate and, therefore, he's *sure* they should never get a look at the numbers. They get pushed further and further out into a limbo of ignorance.

It doesn't take long for the struggling business owner to get himself into a corner where he can't do anything with a new idea because his energies, talents, resources and time have run out. By maintaining his secrecy, he makes sure there's nobody to give an idea to, nobody, at least, who understands enough about the business to be able to do something effective.

Even when and if the owner-manager decides he should open up a little with the employees, his custom-built accounting system just won't let him. When he started, he did his "accounting" on the back of an envelope and Momma did the payroll. There wasn't a lot of need for complicated systems of accounts and financial statements in the beginning.

But he keeps adapting the growing business to this inadequate accounting system by turning the whole thing into an impossible maze. Instead of a system of accounts designed to give management needed information, he develops a system designed to confuse the IRS, camouflage the results, and obscure the decision process. It's designed for everything *but* management.

ACCOUNTING IS A TEACHING TOOL

One of the best management education tools available to a business owner is an accounting system that's tailored specifically and carefully for the business. It's also the best language there is for talking about what is happening to and in the business. But the founder usually ignores this tool--and education altogether. His idea of "need to know" is "you need to know that if you don't work harder, you bum, you're not going to keep your job." He's like the stripper who knows if she takes it *all* off, she'll spend the night in the cooler, so to protect herself, she stands on the stage bumping and grinding in an overcoat and hipboots.

Without a well designed accounting system, the business owner has only two choices, both of them extreme. Like the incompetent stripper, he can either take all his cover off or take nothing off.

What he needs is to ask the most competent accountant he can find how he can reveal his financial facts selectively. What he needs is the ability to present the right data in the right quantity at the right time to generate the greatest participation and anticipation among the managers. What he *does* instead is enshrine his experience. Instead of information his key people get dogma, a dogma that's often more and more out-of-date.

It's true that between the one-truck, one-shovel, one-product days of the start up and the heady positive cash flow of eventual success, lies a lot of experience--good and bad. But most of it is circumstantial. Management skill is developed on a haphazard schedule usually just a little behind the various crises that occur.

Despite this "fuzziness" of experience, the business owner tells heirs and managers: "When you've had my experience, you'll understand." He runs the business exactly the way he always has, slapping down suggestions for changes in product, market, management practice, accounting, promotion, or even the arrangement of the office furniture.

Since the founder *has* been around longer than anyone else, and since he made the money in the first place, who is there to question him? Who, in fact, has any idea what the facts are? Those who have the courage (or imprudence) to question him need only make their inevitable mistakes and his response is: "See, I knew you didn't understand."

The outcome is predictable when the boss is the only one who learns. He tends to become smarter and smarter, while "the help" becomes relatively dumber and dumber. He's the one who usually belongs to the trade associations, goes to the seminars, and reads what few trade magazines are read. By osmosis, if by no other means, he is learning while his management team in the same time frame suffers from denial, inhibition, a spreading case of parochialism, and a growing fear of change. A sound accounting system can help arrest this creeping disease.

When is a business big enough to need a good orthodox accounting system? I'd say almost immediately, because if you don't ever have a sound accounting system, you'll probably never realize you need one. The beginnings of an accounting system, designed to help in understanding the business, should appear the day the doors are opened.

THE FAILURE TO ORGANIZE

To the average business founder, the concept of the real and visible organization chart is about as foreign as most of those abstract paintings that hang in museums. While an organization chart may be second nature to most professionals and managers in large corporations, the business owner thinks it's a bureaucratic frill. His smugness is dangerous. An accurate organization chart, constantly updated as the company changes, is critically important to the proper growth of a business.

A chart is not just an exercise. It's not a venture into commercial art. It's not even there to make the managers feel good about where The Boss puts them. The objective of developing a useful organization chart is to define exactly who is involved in the business--the managers, the advisors, the directors, the shareholders, and the family--and to define their relationships to each other, relationships which tend to overlap and intertwine like worms in a bait can. But this kind of chart seldom exists in a family-owned company.

I'm no longer surprised when organization charts drawn by different protagonists in the same company have only the company name in common. In one case I recall well two brothers, who inherited a business in equal parts, each drew a chart for me on which the other brother was left off. And you absolutely wouldn't believe some of the organization charts the inactive women members of the family in business have drawn for me.

The lines of authority on the chart of the average family-owned company tend to take two basic forms. The first is what I call the *spider* form of organization chart, where the Boss/President/Owner sits in the middle of a series of radiating lines. Spider organizations aren't usually drawn that way--everybody seems to know enough to draw the Boss at the top and then everybody else somewhere below him--but they *exist* in concept nevertheless.

The trademark of the spider organization is the fact that none of the lines of authority touch or cross each other. What happens is the owner-manager, personally, supervises each manager. He talks to each individually. There are no meetings. Nobody gets together to discuss plans or strategy or even problems. Instead, the discussions are held one-on-one, owner-manager to employee-manager. The Boss is in control. Everybody else hangs immobile and solitary in the web, awaiting his summons in a state of suspended animation.

The second common form of organization is what I call the *rake*. In this setup, the lines touch and cross on the chart, but the real flow of authority goes another way. Up at the top of the system is the Boss. Way down at the bottom, like tines on a rake are the "help," usually all spread out on the same level. In between, somewhere in the system, you can bet there's a locked drawer, a closed safe, and the little old lady with the moustache who's hiding the books. As I said earlier, her real function is to keep The Help dumber than The Boss.

Spiders and rakes develop out of the severe pressures of the startup. The reason the books are guarded in the early days is that fact that the Boss is the only person the Boss can really

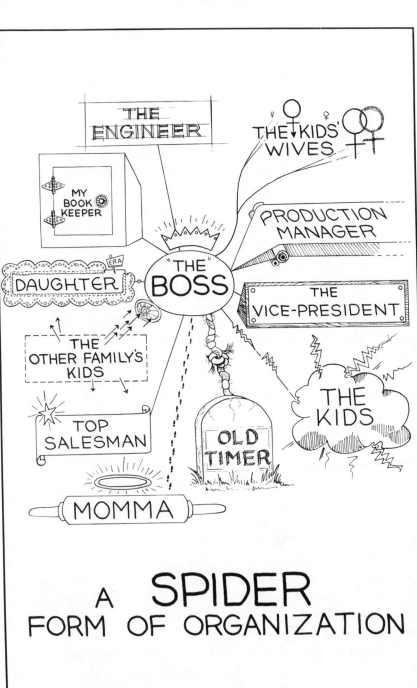

trust with the horrible secret of his "illiquidity." The advisors to the new business have been around since the beginning because it is, in fact, the beginning. The early board is made up of family because nobody has any time--or use--for a real board. Since there are only a few employees, a complex hierarchy is impractical in the beginning.

What's unfortunate about these haphazard designs is that they *remain* , no matter how the business changes. The spider spins more spokes or the rake widens out by getting more tines. (The length of the handle is a function of the boss's social conscience. It's considered more democratic to make it a short handle.) Even though all the original reasons for being webs or rakes are gone because of growth and success, the organization fails to change. Why? Because that's the way the Boss does things...always has. This kind of uninspired organization, based on the hectic and desperate days of the start up, is another bomb lying in the foundation of the growing business.

Later when "the kids" start joining the company right out of school, there are only two job categories--the help who do the work, and the boss who fixes what they do or don't do. So when the kids join there is rarely a need for them. But they have to work somewhere, so Dad takes them under his wing and the chart starts developing warts, spokes, wavy lines, and squiggles. And reserved for the sons-in-law are the dotted lines leading into even lower level indeterminate jobs. (After all, what if the gorilla the owner's baby's sleeping with leaves her and the grandkids?)

When I work with business owners, I usually ask them to show me their charts, knowing full well that most of them don't *have* one. When they admit they don't have a chart, I ask them to draw one, *ad lib* as they see the company. This freehand aboriginal art is as useful to me for diagnosing problems as blood pressure readings, and X-rays are to a physician. How that owner-manager sees and organizes his company is the ink blot test of his business. I've seen literally thousands of these charts and most of them look alike.

The *board of directors* , for example, will usually be made up

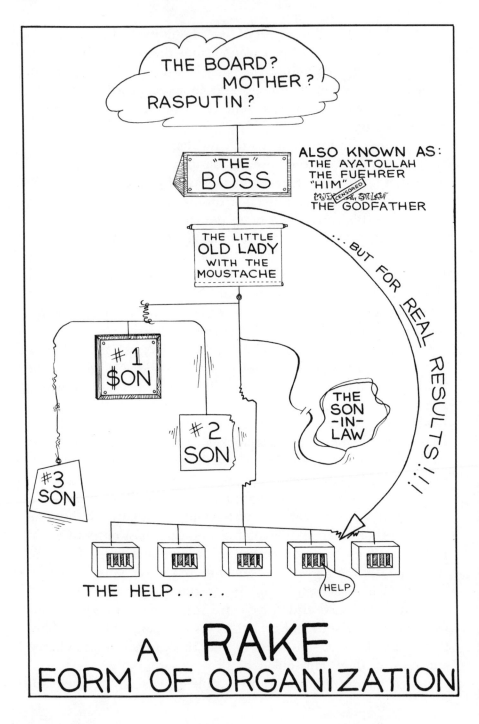

of the founder/owner/president, of course, who is also the chairman; his wife; one or two of the working children (if they're of age); and the company attorney.

The family's on the board for three reasons. One, because the law requires directors; two, because they are convenient and pliable; and, three, because they have (or have potential for) ownership. The attorney is on the board because someone has to put together the minutes of meetings that never happen, in legal form, so that decisions that aren't made can stick. The founder usually finds a second rate lawyer and makes a third rate novelist out of him.

Sometimes there are variations on this basic theme. In corporate partnerships, for example, it's two, or three, or four of everything, depending on the number of partners.

In the event that the partners aren't "equal" for some reason, it's like horse and rabbit stew--one horse, many rabbits, but it mostly tastes like horse.

Often, either for nostalgia's sake or to get a little reinforcement, the owner will install old buddies, influential relatives ("influential" because of marital or minority ownership), or grateful loyal employees (who won't argue because they don't want to turn into ungrateful, disloyal, ex-employees), or company advisors (to assure compliance with the boss' pronouncements).

Such directorships usually only serve either 1) to obscure the director's (and possibly the owner-manager's) incompetence, or 2) to provide legal, though incestuous, sanctions for fee-paid activities, because the owner thinks erroneously it's a cheap way to get advice he would otherwise have to pay for.

Whatever the variation, most boards of directors in most family companies are rubber stamp bodies that make very dubious contributions to the company's well being.

I always ask the person drawing the chart to list the credentials, the ages and length of service of each of the *advisors*

Commonly, they share both age and tenure with the owner-manager, indicating they jumped on board in the early years under less than ideal circumstances, and that they remain

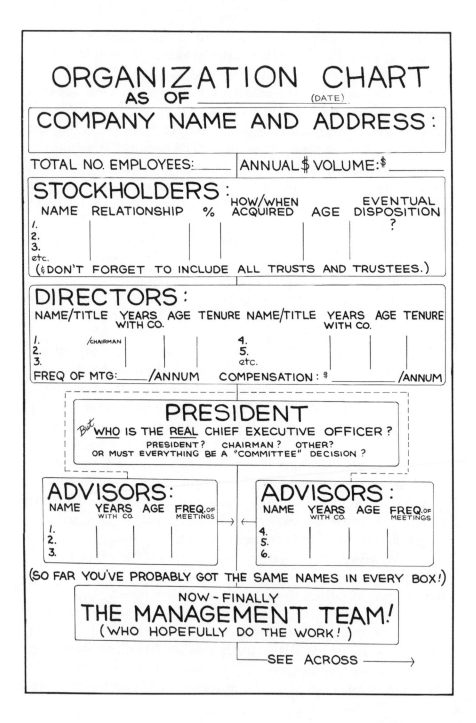

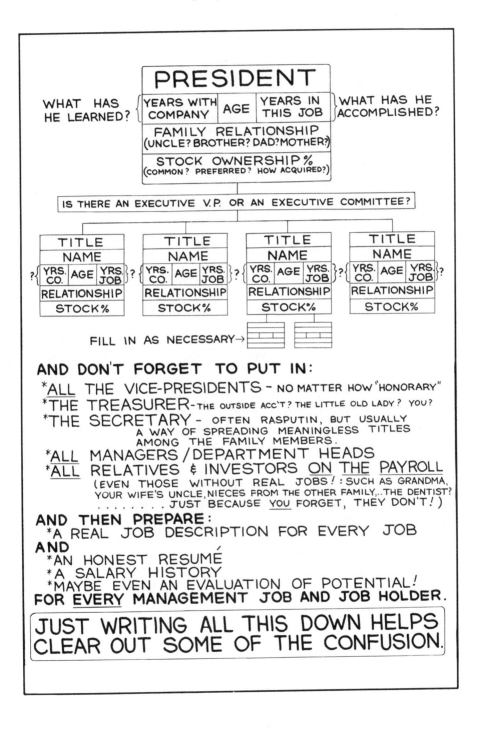

PRESIDENT

WHAT HAS HE LEARNED?

| YEARS WITH COMPANY | AGE | YEARS IN THIS JOB |

WHAT HAS HE ACCOMPLISHED?

FAMILY RELATIONSHIP
(UNCLE? BROTHER? DAD? MOTHER?)

STOCK OWNERSHIP %
(COMMON? PREFERRED? HOW ACQUIRED?)

IS THERE AN EXECUTIVE V.P. OR AN EXECUTIVE COMMITTEE?

TITLE	TITLE	TITLE	TITLE
NAME	NAME	NAME	NAME
YRS. CO. / AGE / YRS. JOB	YRS. CO. / AGE / YRS. JOB	YRS. CO. / AGE / YRS. JOB	YRS. CO. / AGE / YRS. JOB
RELATIONSHIP	RELATIONSHIP	RELATIONSHIP	RELATIONSHIP
STOCK %	STOCK %	STOCK %	STOCK %

FILL IN AS NECESSARY →

AND DON'T FORGET TO PUT IN:

*ALL THE VICE-PRESIDENTS – NO MATTER HOW "HONORARY"
*THE TREASURER – THE OUTSIDE ACC'T? THE LITTLE OLD LADY? YOU?
*THE SECRETARY – OFTEN RASPUTIN, BUT USUALLY A WAY OF SPREADING MEANINGLESS TITLES AMONG THE FAMILY MEMBERS.
*ALL MANAGERS / DEPARTMENT HEADS
*ALL RELATIVES & INVESTORS ON THE PAYROLL
(EVEN THOSE WITHOUT REAL JOBS! : SUCH AS GRANDMA, YOUR WIFE'S UNCLE, NIECES FROM THE OTHER FAMILY,.. THE DENTIST? .... JUST BECAUSE YOU FORGET, THEY DON'T!)

AND THEN PREPARE:

*A REAL JOB DESCRIPTION FOR EVERY JOB
AND
*AN HONEST RESUMÉ
*A SALARY HISTORY
*MAYBE EVEN AN EVALUATION OF POTENTIAL!
FOR EVERY MANAGEMENT JOB AND JOB HOLDER.

JUST WRITING ALL THIS DOWN HELPS CLEAR OUT SOME OF THE CONFUSION.

advisors--at least partially--out of inertia.

Having been around from the beginning is by no means an indictment of these people. But it does raise an eyebrow or two, as well as one very important question: is their *present* contribution up to the *present* needs of the business? Among their credentials should be a client list in whose membership one could take pride.

Organization charts should be prepared every year. They're a powerful personal audit, a management x-ray, a time-lapse study of the spreading family tree, and a useful shareholder geneology. They can serve as pictures of the future, making it easier to predict who will be where, down the road, as the organization ages and grows.

An honest, accurate chart can be used to project the family power structure and to explore important questions. Who owns the business now, in what percentages? Who will become the "instant" owners when those shares are spread around to wives, partners, minority owners, multiple children and their spouses?

The chart can help the owner-manager recognize the existence of all these people and what they want from the future. Do they really understand and share his goals, his hopes, his objectives and his dreams--or do they just feel entitled to get something from him?

The fundamental question to be asked *from the beginning* is whether the business is evolving the way it should. A real organization chart can help answer this question...while there is still time to make the necessary changes if the answer is "no."

An annual review of the organization as the business grows doesn't guarantee anything will change, but it will at least show up the fact that nothing has, and maybe *that* will inspire change.

FAILURE TO ANTICIPATE SUCCESS

Nobody starts a business with the idea they're going to fail. Most entrepreneurs, in fact, have an overblown picture of how smooth their road to success is going to be. Business founders expect to succeed, to the point of studiously ignoring almost overwhelming odds against them, *but what they fail to anticipate is what success will demand* . They just don't plan to meet those demands.

The elimination of secrecy, the development of managers, and constant reorganization to meet the requirements of growth, are important preparations for success, but an equally major consideration in that planning process must involve the education of the owner's *family* , particularly his children.

Raising our children is one of the most important and difficult jobs we will ever have to face. When we also own a business, that job becomes even bigger, because life can be a disaster for a rich kid who grows up with privileges and authority and no real idea what *responsibility* for the ownership of the source of his wealth means.

Usually our children go through their first 100 months of life at about the same time their father is going through his first 100 months as an entrepreneur. If both Dad and the kids get through this process in good shape, respect, understanding and accommodation will be much more likely later.

But what usually happens? Think back. Dad comes home from the office and everything has gone wrong. The IRS is coming on Thursday. The union organizer is dropping by on Friday. The help won't work and business is lousy. Over a drink, he sits down and tells the kids how the competitors are no damn good, how the suppliers won't deliver, how the customers won't pay, and how the government is taking what little he has left. And then Dad puts his arm around his kid and says, "And someday, son, this will all be yours." No wonder the social work looks so appealing--almost anything would.

If this unconscious poison doesn't come from Dad, it comes from Mom when Dad is trying to sell something to someone out of town. "Isn't it a shame," she says. "Our Daddy's out there working so hard, while we have to be all alone eating this casserole." The kids don't have any idea what their father is doing--or why--but they know whatever it is, it's making their mother unhappy.

She's lonely and it's a natural out. I'm not being critical about this. I'm merely telling you what I've observed--and done. I can lose as many points as any other business owner for how many nights I've spent away from home while our kids were growing up.

Dad's just too busy doing, so Mom has her hands full playing both parental roles just trying to raise the kids to be decent human beings. But where else can our children--and later their spouses, and our grandchildren--learn about business and our economic world? How can they learn to understand, to accept, and to share? Only from us.

RAISING RICH KIDS

As early as possible children must understand what their families do. They must understand and accept what they do as *good*...for them, and for those people around them for whom they are responsible. These attitudes are crucial if our children, the raw material of succession, are to *want* to accept our responsibility.

Time must be set aside. A little precious time must be taken to explain *what Daddy does* , to demonstrate... that Daddy loves his business, and *that Mommy loves Daddy enjoying his business*. Whatever Daddy does, it's the source of pleasure, not pain.

This requires a sharing of the dream. This requires that we take every opportunity available to us, for as often as these chances are with us, to communicate as a family, to be understood as a family, and--if we're fortunate--to be accepted as a family.

The founder's children, don't notice his self-destructiveness in the beginning, mainly because they hardly notice him, he's around so seldom. It's only later, as they enter their teens, that they begin to see the signs of wear in their father. By this time, they're more or less conscious, responsible human beings. They're anything but stupid.

They watch their father toiling like a pre-union stevedore, they hear their mother begging him to slow down, to not hit the sauce so hard, to take care of himself. They see him collapse into his chair at night and fall asleep watching TV, still in his working clothes. They see him gaining weight or losing weight, but surely getting out of shape, looking harried and harassed. They see very little, if anything, of his joy in his work.

Yet, if you asked *him*, he would tell you he was setting an example for his kids, that he's instilling in them respect for the work ethic, and the understanding that only hard work can make what you want to come true. He will tell you that since they have it so much better than he did when he was starting out, it's even more important that they learn to respect hard work, that life consists of black bread as well as white bread, and that kids with too much white bread become bums when they grow up.

What *they* see, however, is a man they love destroying himself for reasons they just can't understand. They see many other men, who seem to be equally successful in their eyes, who aren't chewing up their bodies with overwork and overindulgence. They don't understand, and he doesn't help them understand, because he doesn't *know* they don't understand. The circle of misunderstanding can grow wider and wider as the years go by, until it becomes almost impossible for these potential successors to see anything attractive about joining their father's business and the family fights begin.

THE FIRST 100 MONTHS

Between birth and his eighth year, a child must learn to understand four concepts: (1) *love* , (2) *discipline* , (3) *respect* , and (4) *accommodation* . If we can teach those the first 100 months, we can anticipate greater odds in our favor for the future. Kids are like sponges--they soak up whatever surrounds them.

LOVE: A two or three-year-old child is not capable of understanding what his father does, but he can sense when what Daddy does or doesn't do makes Mommy sad. He notices if Mommy's lonesome or Daddy's always gone. He can notice, whenever Daddy happens to be home, that whatever his father does makes him grouchy.

A child may not be consciously aware of what he's feeling--but don't ever doubt that he's feeling. And the bad things that happen in the early years can translate themselves later into an attitude that the business is no damn good, that it's evil. I've heard it far too often: "The kids want nothing to do with the business." Or conversely, that it's just a family cow--to provide milk for the kids without contribution.

If the business owner loves his business, the only way his children will know it is if he shares his own feelings. If he fails to do this, 30 years later, when he is ready to pass the baton, his heirs will be off photographing rocks in California, selling equipment for IBM, or teaching school in Appalachia...anything but working with him in his business.

DISCIPLINE: The lesson of *discipline* is the knowledge that some things *have to be done* , that they can't be postponed. Discipline means that right is right and wrong is wrong. It's having a sense of ethics, of propriety, a sense of integrity, and a sense of priority. These can really only be learned by example or sad experience.

Our business can offer a great life, but our heirs must learn very early, from our own actions, that there are standards of performance. They must see that things can't always be put off, that benefit can only follow from contribution. Without this, they will find it impossible to muster up the energy and commitment that will be demanded of them by the business in the years to come. (Or as my Grandmother used to say, "Freedom comes as the fruit of self-discipline.")

RESPECT: We all too easily talk in front of our heirs about cheating the IRS or conning the creditors. But we have to remember from the *beginning* that our example will provide them their earliest standards of the respect, compassion, understanding, or trust we feel it proper to hold in order to succeed.

What a price we pay for unguarded comments about our employees, our partners and their family, about our customers, suppliers, and competitors. How satisfying it is at dinner to spice up adult conversation with descriptions of how employees are lazy, or stupid, or irresponsible. We talk about our customer's cupidity and unworthiness. We discuss our supplier's lack of ethics or integrity. It goes on and on.

All of this shows us our "sophistication." It makes us feel good, clever, flawless. But remember who's listening.

Fifteen, 20 years later, that 30-year-old employee we talked about is now 45-50, still working for us, only now he's a vice president. Our children have heard almost from infancy what a lush, or incompetent, or ingrate, whatever, that this man is. And we wonder why this key manager thinks our son or daughter is a smart aleck who shows him no respect.

Fifteen, 20 years later, we wonder why our kids see nothing wrong with cheating a customer (after all, that's what they did to us in the old days), why they're unhappy with long-term suppliers (they never did anything for us), or uncooperative with good industry prospects (why should we go along with them?). That's what they've learned from their great teachers--us.

ACCOMMODATION: The future will be populated with adult versions of the children we raise in the early years. Very few heirs are only children of only children. Usually, there are brothers, sisters, cousins, children of partners--a whole range of "heirs." Each must be treated fairly (though not necessarily equally) and each must understand and accept what is done as "fair" and done out of love.

Training for this must begin as early as the division of toys. We want our children to think well of our business, to respect what it requires and what it gives, and to realize that they must constantly temper their requirements to those of their brothers, sisters, cousins, and everybody else involved. This is the precise opposite of "it's my rattle," or "that's not fair," or "he has more than...." A child's value system, good or bad, is quickly learned--and easily reinforced, and hard to change.

If the dream is not shared this way, the groundwork has been laid for disaster and if *love*, *discipline*, *respect*, and *accommodation* are not learned very early, the danger increases that we will have created unwilling, unworthy, incompetent, or irresponsible heirs.

Just think what they will do when shares of company stock are substituted for toys.

THE SECOND 100 MONTHS

In his second 100 months, the child should *learn the meaning of money*. This major lesson in economics is probably best taught between the ages of 8 and 16. Much before that it's meaningless and much after that, it probably won't take.

Unfortunately, it's on this subject that people are most likely to harm their children, either because they treat money the way the Victorians treated sex--as something everybody had but never discussed--or else they take the other extreme and talk about nothing *but* money.

Our children must learn that money per se is not evil, that property and privilege are generally earned through dedication and hard, honest work. They can learn, by our example, that the uses of money are a necessary and even enjoyable part of life.

They cannot, nor should they, be shielded from its existence or given shallow answers.

Our children will be inheriting our wealth. What else are we going to do with it? Give it all to charity? Our feuds with the IRS, in fact, are mainly over ways to make our heirs richer. Our success has created wealth that we are going to have to distribute. We can't take it with us and most of us probably don't have either the conscience or the ingenuity to be able to consume it all.

But to pass on wealth, power and the means of influencing other people's lives, without also sharing the sense of responsibility that must go with that wealth and power, is like handing a loaded gun to the unstable. We are responsible for our actions. If we can't handle it, our actions will only strengthen the arguments of those critics who say we should not have the right to pass a heritage on to our children.

Understanding that our wealth and privilege were earned can help our heirs feel comfortable with the wealth they'll inherit. One of two questions come up again and again at our seminars among young members of families in business: "Is it *fair* to have so much money when so many others don't have it?" or conversely, "Why can't I flaunt it, it's going to be mine?"

We might as well ask why some people have more or better health or beauty or athletic ability. These also seem to be inequitably distributed gifts.

Nobody can control the initial distribution of good fortune. There is always an element of chance involved in that. But to enjoy, appreciate, and build on what privileges and benefits we're given, we must work.

We can be born with health, but we must work to keep it. We may have athletic skills, but without training they become useless. We can have a chance at education, but we must study to get it. We can inherit wealth, but unless we use it and manage it wisely, it will eventually disappear. If money alone is all we inherit, it leaves much to be desired.

Our children can and must learn to respect what benefits and privileges they have. We must teach them to be comfortable with money without being smug about it. They must understand what it can do and what it is for. If they can't manage their own affairs by their mid-teens, what can we expect them to do with the rest of our money when they inherit it?

Some people say that children should earn any money they spend to learn "self reliance." I would feel much better if children could learn *responsibility* . How do you teach that to children who will undoubtedly inherit substantial sums when they have never learned to handle money until too late.

A very successful father I know gave his children a check book of their own at 12 years of age and deposited to their account the sums expended in their behalf for lessons, doctors fees, education, books, trips, clothes, etc. Fifteen years later his children were far better money managers than their contemporaries who never were exposed.

With patience, skill, commitment, and the grace of God's help, by the time our children finish their second 100 months they can have discipline, they can love and be able to accommodate others in their family. They can respect the contribution of others and enjoy the feeling of knowing what their family business does and why it is their father's dream. They can be comfortable with responsibility, while having a well-developed respect for money and what it can do.

THE THIRD 100 MONTHS

During the last 100 months of our children's learning period, the years 16 to 25, they must now add to their prior understanding by learning their value to themselves and to the world. They have to learn this realistically. This means a *job* , preferably a job working for somebody else..

Naturally we all want our children to have money, to have comforts, but the way to do this is not, say, to pay them $6.75 an hour to paint the stripes in the company parking lot, just because that's the going rate to our labor force. That doesn't teach the economic value of labor and ability. Better to pay them a realistic $3-4 an hour or have them work for somebody else and give them the extra $2-3-5 as a gift, to apply to their needs with our love.

The business owner--or more likely, his tax advisors--can come up with all kinds of tax reasons for overpaying our kids for minimal work they never did. But saving on taxes and beating Uncle Sam out of his share (deserved or undeserved) is no reason to ruin our children. It's almost an unwritten law: cheat the tax collector and spoil the child.

Children are not born with an understanding of what they can do or what they are worth to others. They surely won't have any idea what the world expects of them unless we make sure that they find out. And they'll find this out best in the hands of objective outsiders. If at all possible, we should try to postpone bringing our heirs right away into the family business--they *deserve* a chance to learn about themselves on their own by getting their first jobs from somebody else.

There are two significant benefits to this. First, it will allow the young man or woman the opportunity to collect credentials in the eyes of the non-family employees. It won't hurt their image in the eyes of the family either. Second, working for somebody else can develop a powerful appreciation for the benefits and value of the family business.

The first 300 months are critical. These lessons are the lessons we must teach to our children. It is a critical responsibility, because when heirs to a business are unprepared, money can become a set of loaded pearl-handled pistols with common stock for bullets. If our heirs aren't properly taught, then those fights over the rattle become fights for control--a battle few businesses can afford or survive.

In the best of all possible worlds if we do everything right, we can approach our 60's with mature heirs who share our mutual respect and who possess discipline, confidence, experience, and maybe even some wisdom.

THE WIFE'S KEY ROLE

Obviously, another major ingredient in this teaching process is the founder's wife. She is the person who is raising that next generation, because her husband works so much and seldom is home when the kids aren't sleeping.

This places an additional teaching responsibility on the founder. He must share as much as he can with his children, of course, but while he's doing so, he must also share with his partner...his wife. She must understand. She must be accepted by her husband as the powerful ally that she can be.

From the beginning, he should take a litle bit of time every day to talk to his wife about the dream. Even if she is working in the business, she is too often working as an employee, not as a partner. She needs to understand. She wants--and needs--to have some sense of control over her destiny and her future.

Most of all, she wants to be a help and an encouragement to the man she married. She wants and needs to *share* .

From the day the founder sees his business off the ground he should constantly be asking himself whether the business he started will, in fact, continue. If it will, as he surely hopes, can it continue the way it has been going?--is going? Is he laying the groundwork for a successful growing, continuing business, or is he simply planting little bombs all over the company lot, bombs that will blow up later, when he is expecting to reap his harvest and his heirs are ready to take their opportunity?

The future, whatever it becomes, is the founder's responsibility. Even the ancient Greeks knew this, thousands of years ago:

"If I could get to the highest place in Athens, I would lift my voice and say, 'What mean you, fellow citizens, that you turn every stone to scrape wealth together, and take so little care of your children, to whom you must one day relinquish all?'"

II

THE TRANSITION

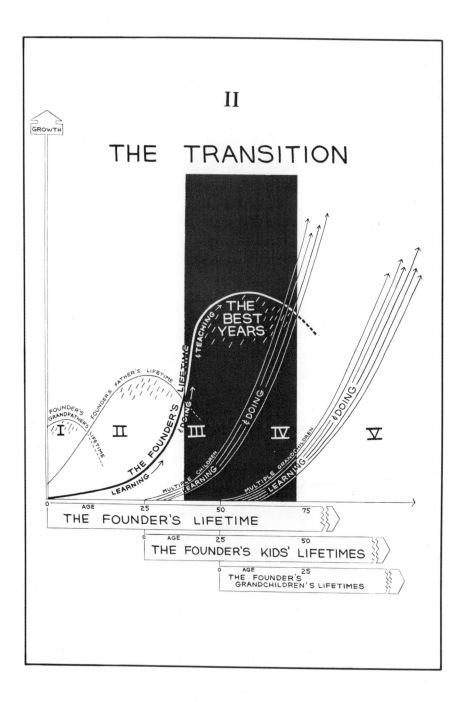

II

THE TRANSITION

Chapter 5

Someone with Enough: the Business Owner

Eventually the business catches hold. Assuming the founder is one of the winners, his business becomes successful far beyond what he dared expect. It also becomes bigger than he expected. The up-front costs paid in the beginning are taking their toll. Dad and Mom realize what they've missed. Problems within the business seem intractable. The need for new ideas, for new abilities, for growth are all becoming obvious, but this means WORK...and Dad feels he's worked long and hard enough.

Now the days of the start up are past. Time has gone by, maybe 15 or 20 or 30 years, and the struggling entrepreneur has emerged from his garage or his basement or his attic to stand in the full light of day as a "business owner."

When he started out, he was in business for himself, but now, with success, he has become a private, independent businessman, by God. He is one of the winners--one of the few winners. He survived the battle while the losers were all shot out of the water. He can see the future and it no longer looks bleak. He has entered the foothills of his indulgent years.

He is a power in his community, envied by his neighbors, indulged by his suppliers, and treated with decency by his customers. The town is grateful for his payroll. The relatives are thankful for his largess. To his competitors, he's become a force to reckon with.

In his eyes and in the eyes of most of the world he *makes* it. He looks successful. He goes to conventions, lies to his suppliers, and drinks with his competitors. He becomes *divine* and pontificates on everything from celibacy in the clergy to housekeeping in resort hotels. Then suddenly, one day, along with *divinity* comes *immortality* . (I'll never forget the fellow who said to me one day, "Now, Doc, *if* I should die...", like he had a choice.)

It's natural, once you assume you're immortal, to forget about the future. Hell, the future is infinite. Why think about it? But this *assumed immortality* has probably visited more havoc on family-owned businesses than anything that could be done to them by competitors, tax laws, labor unions, or inflation.

At this point it also begins to occur to the founder that he's suffered long enough. He's been denying himself for too long, cutting paper napkins in half, wearing the same shirt two-three days in a row, flying night coach, and bringing hotel soap home from his trips for too long. He's cut enough corners. He discovers his growing wealth like the boy who suddenly discovered that he could talk to girls.

His self-indulgence isn't outrageous right away. That takes a while. But he learns.

THE FAMILY ENTERS THE FAMILY BUSINESS

It also occurs to him that he has these children he has to think about. When they were little, they were Momma's problem and a comfort to him on weekends. But now they're in their teens or early twenties, and they're asking questions, or thinking about college, and just generally becoming functioning *economic* entities. They're hard to ignore.

The "venture" that was started as a way to keep the sheriff from the door, to feed the kids three times a day, and to make payments on the house, the TV set and the car, now suddenly has become a "family business" (See Chapter 6).

The business has substance, almost a life of its own, and the founder begins taking an entirely different view of his baby. His success inevitably changes his needs and alters his goals. He is well "Beyond Survival." He's beyond security. He's got status. He feels reasonably well satisfied. Now what?

He's entering an entirely new world in which, again, he has no experience. The needs of the business and the needs of the business owner now begin to conflict. He is nearing his destination and unconsciously has started gathering up his packages so he can get off at his stop. He's entering the prelude to the flat growth curve.

He thinks about private schools for his kids, taking vacations south in the wintertime instead of going to state parks, and flying first class. He has money and he's becoming aware of the fact that so many of the better things in life can be made deductible.

He looks at his salary and wonders whether he should maybe take more out in expenses and less in salary, because then it only costs half of what it used to cost. He begins losing the kind of respect he had for money in the early years.

This is the beginning of the good life, of becoming a better consumer as well as a bigger producer. It's also the time when his children, the heirs, are at their most susceptible age. Too often, he gives them anything they want just so they'll stay out of his hair. They tend to be unbridled and can begin to become unmanageable.

The restraints of poverty are being removed from the founder and all there is to keep him together are the restraints of his upbringing--his faith, his ethnic culture, his mother's knee, and his own father's homilies of virtue: "Son, never use cheap leather," "only go first class," "don't borrow on the come," and "never swing on the second pitch."

The business owner and his family begin to move into different relationships in the community. They are making more money than their friends and relatives. They associate with different people because of added resources and freedom, as well as because of the new and different requirements put on them by the growing business.

They move to a better neighborhood, drink a better grade of booze, join the best country club, buy a diesel sedan. And all of it is difficult. If they don't handle these changes with sensitivity and understanding, they can become dominated by guilt or resentment. If these changes are difficult for Mom and Dad, who are now in their forties or fifties, imagine what it must be like for their growing and impressionable children.

The founder is at the peak of his doing years, the period of his greatest accomplishments, the top of his wave. His family is pretty well set. He has all of the children he will probably have, and they are starting to be known as the rich kids in town. His family become neighborhood migrants, moving upward. And as they move, they join the clubs, make their contacts, acquire expensive tastes. He rises in his industry and in his association. Everything he touches turns to gold--gold which, later, he will spend most of his time polishing.

NEW REASONS FOR SECRECY

I don't see the founder early in this stage. He doesn't call me. He doesn't come to our seminars. He's too busy being a big shot, a *secretive* big shot.

In the beginning, remember, he was secretive because there was nobody he could trust with all the little things he had to do to survive. But now, with success and his newly discovered affluence, he starts worrying about being misunderstood. He begins to acquire a lot of things which are legally and properly his, but which have a tendency to embarrass him in front of others. Sometimes he hides the good crystal when friends from the past come to visit.

His salary is pretty high--or at least he thinks it would seem so in the eyes of his employees. I'm really working hard, he tells himself, like a dog. I just have to get away to that convention in Hawaii, Puerto Rico, Bermuda, even though business is terrible. I'm doing everything I can, but they won't understand. In the old days, "business is terrible" meant that there wasn't enough cash to meet the payroll. At this point, however, it's come to mean breaking even. The problem is that it takes an increasingly creative accounting system to keep breaking even...higher and higher.

Because he doesn't have an organization chart, it's almost impossible for him to design an accounting system that lets him give his people their part of the whole without explaining "too much." Either he's naked or he's covered. So he stays covered and gets used to it.

He worries about competitors finding out what he's doing. If they find out he's doing X dollars in this area, then, boy, they're going to see that it's a market and come in and do it better. He doesn't want his suppliers to know that he is profitable, because then they are going to want to raise the price. He's afraid he'll lose his ability to negotiate if anybody knows what he's really doing.

People would take advantage of him. Employees would want a raise. The relatives would want a handout. His wife would want more time. So he stays inarticulate, and the business is kept just disorganized enough so that it's impossible for data to be presented in a logical way to anybody. His motto is: "Don't tell 'em nuttin'."

THE "CONTROLLED GROWTH" FANTASY

As he nears his goals, he tries to speed everything up. This is the time of "just a little bit more." He thinks, boy, another half million dollars in sales and I could do this or that. Growth becomes a consuming addiction. He wants leverage from borrowed money, but there's a limit to how much people will lend him--either his suppliers, through credit, or bankers through loans. The last thing he wants, of course, are equity partners. So the only other source of funds for the business are the customers. That's called "growth," the simple dollar increase in size.

But what happens is he gets the whole thing going too fast. He passes up his stop because he *can't* stop. As he grows, as he gets that other half million, he begins to discover that his cash flow just doesn't carry the investment. It's a simple principle his accountant would have explained to him if he'd asked. Or maybe he just didn't listen. In any event, he soon learns that the cash flow requirements are usually greater than the immediate growth returns.

But *returns* are what he wants. What he wants are tax free benefits. He wants the business to be efficient. He wants to keep the money rather than invest any more in capital assets. He wants to keep raising prices, to put no more into the product and keep a high variable return by keeping his fixed costs low and constant.

After suffering this dilemma for a while, he begins to feel that growth seems to be self-defeating. It eventually dawns on him that he really doesn't want to grow anymore. The "entrepreneur" in the business founder phases out in the face of the prospect of more sacrifice and more damn hard work.

The founder starts putting on the brakes. He stops expanding except on sure things. He wants to have the order in the bank before he builds the building, and even then he wants to leverage it. He wants, purely and simply, to stop growing.

He's reached 50 or 55 or 60 and in the back of his mind is this growing desire for some peace and quiet. He wants to live better. He wants to enjoy things, to take a little time off. These thoughts are in the back of his mind long before the effects start showing up in the business, but once the seeds are planted, the tendency grows. He starts to rationalize the concept of "controlled growth."

This is what starts to flatten out the growth curve in the family-owned business. It's not the absence of market or motivated managers or talented successors or money, at least not directly. It's the founder's lack of tolerance for risk. It typically happens in businesses which have many ways they could grow. They just don't. The GNP has nothing to do with it. The tax laws have little to do with it. *It's the deliberate ignoring of opportunity.*

He asks himself a reasonable question: why risk what I have for more of what I don't want--worry, anxiety, work, harassment? He starts to become "efficient" instead of effective, to think only in the present, ignoring the future--as though he weren't going to be living in it.

The owner-founder retires on the job, but usually unconciously, and completely unknown to him or anyone else and in ways that are unintelligible to the outsider. As his growth curve flattens, he rides a wave that looks like success. He keeps more and enjoys more--but he's eating his bait.

NOT WITH HIS MONEY

He's collecting his receivables faster than he's generating them. His capital investment is lower than his depreciation. He worries about returns on certificates of deposit. The IRS is after him for 531 problems, (Section 53l of the Internal Revenue Code deals with "unreasonable" accumulation of "surplus" funds.) and when his managers suggest that energies and funds be spent in new areas, he says "not with my money, you don't." He really wants to hold back the dawn.

Try to tell him he's doing this and he'll probably punch you in the mouth, but at some point,the successful business owner retires on the job because he really doesn't need it anymore. At least he doesn't need money enough for it to remain as a growth inducement or a motivator.

I get too many questions like: "Why do we *have* to grow?" for this not to be true.

This change in the business founder is profound. In the beginning, he never heard of such a thing as "controlling" growth. Then he wanted all he could take of it, and he'd take anything. But inevitably, with success, his personal consumption begins to fall behind his production and he begins to wonder why he needs more.

CHANGE IS INEVITABLE

Understandable as this question may be, it arises from a dangerous delusion--the founder's conviction that because *he* doesn't want change that change won't occur. The purpose of growth is not to get bigger. Growth is just another way of saying that the inevitable changes will be in a positive direction.

But because few things generate cash faster than a declining business, it's easy for the successful founder to come to the conclusion that growth only *decreases* profitability, while at the same time increasing his workload and forcing him to undergo many of the same fears and worries he knew in the early years.

This belief is especially strong if the founder is the only person with the dream. If the other people in his life don't accept it, he finds it's so much easier just to say the hell with it, I'll stay where I am.

It is now that some of the little bombs planted in the early days of the business begin to go off. The founder, because of his secretive habits, usually hasn't shared his dream with anybody in his family. He also has failed to invest time and understanding in his children. Just at the time when the best stimulus to continued growth would be managers and successors with whom to do it, people with whom he has mutual respect and trust, he finds himself alone.

The eager student creates the eager teacher. The experience and knowledge needed for growth is within the founder, but the *need* for growth has to come from successor management. It's at this exact point that the weak link leading to the demise of so many family-owned businesses snaps.

Change is inevitable and adaptive growth is necessary if the business is going to survive and provide for the founder's real security, emotional as well as financial. The key to letting it happen is his ability to change his perspective. He's *done* enough. In that feeling, he's justified. Building a successful business is a major accomplishment and takes a lot out of the builder. But both his perspective and his feeling of personal supremacy are unrealistic. The world in which he built his business no longer exists.

The founder can't simply alter his energy level in the prime of his life to keep up with his receding hairline. Instead he has to learn to change from being a *doer* to being a *teacher*.

Learning to teach instead of doing it yourself isn't easy, however, and it's particularly difficult for the business owner. To him there's nobody else who can do things as well as he can. In many senses, he's right about that. In other senses, there are people around him who can do things so much better. He has to learn where to look and what to accept, and not to be so fearful of the future.

The key, I think, is to learn to accept a little bit of "dust."

AN ACCEPTABLE LEVEL OF DUST

My mother, in my opinion, was the world's most dedicated housekeeper. People would be followed with the vacuum, ashtrays whisked away in mid-cigar, my Dad's socks were pressed, and the houseplants polished. That was the world in which I grew up.

Then I got married. I remember one day being bothered by some dust on the piano. It didn't seem right. It drove me crazy. My wife was an RN, and had run an entire hospital floor. She was one of the few people I knew who came close to working harder than I did. But the dust on the piano was unacceptable to me. So I wrote "I love you" in it with my finger.

Well, the house, as always, she kept clean, but she saw to it that my message and the little circle of dust she kept around it stayed on the piano for a couple of months. It took me that long to catch on. I eventually realized that no house is ever completely dust free. It can always be improved, but at some point happiness requires some mutually acceptable level of "dust."

What usually prevents most business owners from delegating, leaving their hands off things, relaxing, and finally retiring, is the inability to accept some dust. They can always see something wrong and they fix it. Other people seem always to leave more dust than they ever did. But what they fail to realize is that others don't do a worse job. They just tend to dust in different places, for different reasons, under different priorities, in different times.

The founder's meddling wouldn't be so serious if it wasn't for the fact that he's reaching the end of his doing years. He's tired. He wants to take it easy. So his meddling isn't just meddling. He comes down on the business like an iron hand that nobody can move.

Sooner or later, someone's going to have to do the founder's job. He can either ensure that they profit from his knowledge and experience or he can see that they don't. That's up to him. But how they actually do the job, assuming they ever get the chance, is really up to them.

The founder finds this hard to accept. Instead, he spends his time looking for--and finding--reasons why he couldn't pass control along even if he wanted to. He finds a multitude of ways to put off his tough decisions, particularly the decisions he faces about himself and his heirs. He puts his company on hold while he waits for things to "work out."

AWAITING THE PRODIGAL

He waits for heirs to get old enough, smart enough, willing enough, or experienced enough--and he waits and waits. Many decisions about management or markets or products just aren't made, as though the world will conveniently stand still until his hopes for solutions become reality. After 20-30-40 years, he's getting tired. And these problems absorb great quantities of energy.

He finds all sorts of rationalizations for delay. If the heirs aren't old enough, well, just give them a little time and they will be. If they don't have any experience, let it ride, they'll pick it up quick enough when they need it. If they're not all that bright, then it's probably best not to do anything at all. If they're nasty or arrogant -- they'll grow out of it.

Meanwhile, the company's pressing needs for competent managers--family members or otherwise--is stubbornly ignored. When I meet business owners in this stage, I often am reminded of the Third Reich waiting for the secret weapon to save their war effort.

For example, one founder I know is developing his secret weapon--his 17-year-old son. He has three children, the oldest two of whom are daughters both happily married to surgeons. His son, the child of a second marriage, is planning to enter college next year.

My friend just celebrated his sixty-third birthday and by

any timetable he should be actively grooming a successor, not only to take over some of the operating responsibilities, but also to take over the executive responsibility for the company in the very near future. But given the facts about his age, the youth of his son, and the lack of interested sons-in-law, this successor would have to be an outsider, at least for the next 15 years or so.

The installation of his son is an event he may not personally witness, but he should have known this and thought about it for 15 years. But unconsciously this thought upsets him--it requires him to contemplate his mortality and the need for some hard decisions and plans for his own remaining years and his family's security. How easy it becomes to blame taxes, government, inflation, whatever, and give up because nothing can be done when it's too late.

My friend can't accept this as a possibility. He wants his son to take over the business as soon as possible and he's afraid that putting an interim outsider in that slot would delay the young man's installation. Most likely he's right. The interim president would naturally expect to hold the job for a reasonable length of time. Few competent men would accept such a position otherwise.

All of these facts added together make his decision a tough one, especially since my friend knows bringing in an outsider as president would require accepting new philosophies and accepting new sources of information. The outsider would want to do things differently. He'd want to invest in new approaches. He'd want to know and *grow* --and probably differently, because he would see things differently.

If this is too much to accept--or if it becomes increasingly plain to all that the son has either (1) no real business aptitude not just in Dad's eyes but viewed by objective outsiders or (2) has very definite and different ideas about his future--then Dad may have to someday consider a sale to employees--or outsiders. Sometimes creating a couple of older "business brothers" is a good interim idea. In fact, there are many alternatives. After all, Dad has known for many years the "facts" in his case--but, like the ostrich, has preferred to hide his head rather than seek help from sources competent to help him.

Most successful business owners are successful because they learned the hard way to be realists. They took a major unknown risk in the beginning when they started the business, mainly because they didn't have any choice, but after that they took continuing risks based on *facts,* on what they *knew*, on what they *expected*. They took *calculated* risks and succeeded.

But when it comes to the future of their business, too many of these same founders tend virtually to ignore all the laws of probability, as well as a whole collection of simple and obvious facts. By doing nothing, they take some of the wildest risks imaginable, and risk destroying in their later years that which they created in their earlier years with such effort.

THE PROBLEMS ONLY GET BIGGER

A growing, successful business has management needs that are continuing. Survival requires change and change requires constant, competent management. There will always be reasons why things may be better tomorrow, why these problems would go away if we could only wait a few years. The trouble is that time continues to pass, and as it passes, it has the unnerving tendency to replace simpler problems with much bigger ones.

The permanent two-martini nirvana the successful business founder looks forward to as his just reward for all the years of toil and sweat is an unworkable pipedream--and in his heart he knows it.

It's unworkable because he is not designed for that kind of end. He became an entrepreneur and succeeded because he has a built-in need to achieve and to build. This internal drive doesn't simply disappear once he becomes successful or older.

It's unworkable because, even if he could stand the years of inactivity and aimlessness that come with milking a successful business, the business couldn't. Not even the most productive cow can be milked forever without requiring some return investment.

A successful family-owned business is a better investment in these trying days than gold, diamonds, stocks, tax frees, or oil. It represents *earning* power, but that earning power will continue only if time, effort, dedication and commitment are invested in the continuity of the business and, therefore, in the people who will make the business work when the founder no longer can.

What the world economy is going to do, where the price of gold is going to be 10-20 years from now, what inflation is going to do to the Dow Jones average, are questions best left to the fortune tellers. The answers are best left to them too.

One thing remains sure, and that is that the founder's problems are only going to be solved by his heirs, by the successors to his dream, whether they are from his family or from someone else's family. This requires that he have some confidence in the future and a willingness to take a risk on chosen successors in whom he has faith.

A RISK WE UNDERSTAND

What better risk is there than one taken on something we understand? What better risk is there than one we can influence, both through our direct efforts and through our ability to transfer our knowldge and experience to others who also understand?

It's this kind of risk that the survival of a successful business demands, and it must be taken or the business will surely die. It will fail, it will be liquidated, it will be sold. And with it will disappear the earning power, the freedom and the opportunity that took so long, and so much hard work, to build.

The successful founder has earned the right to stop *doing*. But what he has also earned is the responsibility to *teach* others so that the business he built can be continued.

Chapter 6

The Founder's Expanding Family

Very seldom is a family in business blessed with only one heir who is both competent and interested in the business. More likely, there are multiple children. Often there are children of partners. Most often, these children have not been taught the essential economic lessons. These relationships seethe beneath the surface, erupting occasionally, making the already unstable situation critical. Questions of fairness and competence arise while Dad and Mom are paralyzed by their love for the children and their fears about their own future. The heirs--who are supposed to be the solution--too often are the problem.

At about this time the successful founder is dreaming wistfully of his nirvana. (In case you haven't figured it out yet, this "nirvana" I refer to so often is that semi-comatose state of Hindu consciousness wherein all is sweetness and light. For most of us, it is an unreal concept *not* to be confused with peace of mind.) He also finds himself looking nervously over his shoulder at his ever-expanding family.

This entrepreneur, who started with little more than a need to find fulfillment and freedom for himself while he somehow fed and clothed his family, reaches success and discovers a bewildering maze of human problems--business and non-business.

Added to the smorgasbord of headaches spread out for him by his growing business is a powerful stew of family conflict. The ability of this steaming cauldron to make its presence known can rival the aroma of boiling cabbage, and there's little question that the whole mess has a recurring tendency to boil over.

It didn't suddenly appear. While the entrepreneur was working through his doing years, the crowd of related people around him--the alter-ego of the business--was growing bigger and more restless with every passing day.

He probably didn't notice them until they organized into rival camps, but eventually it occurs to him that they are an important fact of life which has to be faced up to and accommodated. Feeling the force of their impact over and over, he comes to the often belated conclusion that his future and the future of the business depends on them.

FAMILY BUSINESSES ARE UNIQUE

This is his business *mishpocheh*. I use this Yiddish word for a very good reason. *All* of the people connected to the business through blood or legal ties are important to that business's future, just as much as the blood kin and immediate family. It's unfortunate that English has no good word to describe this collection of brothers, sisters, parents, aunts, uncles, cousins, and other family relations. The *mishpocheh* is the extended family, the tribe, the people who share a common heritage. In the case of the family owned business, this common heritage is the business itself.

These people are the major reason why the successful family-owned business is a special and endangered species.

Many people who have theories on family businesses may attribute their special nature to smaller size or the ability to take advantage of special opportunities--and, naturally, these characteristics *do* make a difference, particularly for the startup business--but they are very far from being the most important factors separating successful family-owned businesses from the public firms.

Family-owned businesses are unique because of the people in them and their relationships with each other. Remember that many of these people are not simply employees or managers or investors. They are *family*. They are *related*. What anywhere else would be simple business concerns become intimately tied up with the unalterable *fact* of "family."

This is what the founder finds out as he reaches his long sought for success. Because of it, he discovers his challenge has only just begun.

Now he discovers he has children. Not the toddlers he used to bounce on his knee when he was home on weekends, but actual *people*, people with increasing needs and growing demands. Partners and investors have children, too, and, while their demands may be a little less acceptable to him, they are also not to be denied.

His children marry other people's children and, together *they* have children of their own to pull on the already confused strings of Grandpa's heart. If the founder remarries, he may have to make room for the children of his second wife's former marriage--and they may have children of their own.

This is all to say nothing about various commitments he made in the past to employees and others who were introduced to "the business." The cast keeps pouring on stage like the characters in a high school variety show.

With the inevitable passage of time, all of these people become crucial actors in the evolving future of the business. They get educated to varying levels and in varying ways. In their exposure to life as they see it, they develop individual attitudes, personalities, tastes, opinions, and spouses.

They become individuals and their relationships show the same kinds of accommodations and disagreements as are found in any family. Only now there's the added amplifier of a family business to help expand everything from simple squabbles into out-and-out warfare.

THE INSTANT FAMILY

Blood ties aren't the only qualifications for this family. There are many people who join the business family from the outside, people who have been raised and greatly influenced by others. The founder doesn't know them. They don't know him.

He may have had a shot at raising his own children to believe and respect what he believes and respects, but the early attitudes of his "instant" family--his sons-in-law, partners, partners' wives and kids, and probably most important, his daughters-in-law--are out of his hands. In Yiddish...these "in-laws" would be called the *machetunim* --relatives by marriage.

To this extended family of relatives and in-laws, one also must add the business "relatives"...the *long-term employees* who are like brothers to the founder because they grew up in the business together, and the *key managers* . In the absence of qualified or interested heirs, these people may be the best available successors. Many a family-owned business was acquired by ambitious employees who, in turn, started a new family business on the legacy of the old.

All of these people--the *family mishpocheh* , the *in-law machetunim* (too often the *out* laws), and the *business relatives* --make up a wider group I call the business "mishpocheh." It is by nature explosive because of its ever-expanding complexity.

As it expands, it picks up an even greater percentage of people whom the founder didn't raise or train. And each time a new person is added, a new and unpredictable pole of influence is brought into the family--usually without recognition.

For the founder, this expanding burlesque usually results in an irresistible pressure to apply his significant, but limited abilities to nonproductive activities. Year after year he may become more embroiled in the internecine warfare, as his family and the management organization gather into varying camps of warring adversaries.

As he struggles with this expanding clatter of arms, he can often begin to lose sight of his business. He can even begin to lose hope--through frustration--that his dream has any future at all.

From the beginning, this extended family of his required the same care and attention that he gave to his products and his customers. If his business settled down and ran well in the success years, it was because he worked at it. The same can be true of his business *mishpocheh* . He reaps what he sows.

This expanding family requires the same care and interest the founder expended on developing his own children for the future, the major difference being that he must develop his instant family a lot smarter and a lot faster. To fail to do so is dangerous, like letting go of a high volume fire hose. Once it gets out of hand it's hard to stop.

I feel it's both unfair and a mistake for the founder to feel that it's none of his business. If he's going to be so smug about taking all the credit for his great and glorious accomplishments, he has to take responsibility for the actions of everybody in his charge.

That's how he won success in the old days. No detail was too insignificant for his attention. It's only when his energy level dwindles that he says "to hell with it." He says it, but he's *not* willing to accept the consequences.

There's no way I could cover the almost infinite variations on this theme, although I begin to feel I've seen them all. The relationships among multiple family members are usually the very core of the problems I've been called upon to help solve, and if I could just convince more people of the absolute importance of understanding the varying needs of the business family, I'd feel that my short time on this earth wasn't wasted.

THE IMPORTANCE TO OUTSIDERS

It's not just a problem faced by the founder. Every member of a family owning a business gets embroiled in the joys and conflicts. Every member shares the same responsibility for whatever conflicts and accommodations may occur.

The business family is important to others, too.

Employees in a family business have to understand that the "kids" are their future managers and security. It often falls on their shoulders to teach and train this next generation, the "nepots," and if they fail to do it with responsibility and dedication, these employees could be sealing their own fate. If the heir can't handle it when the old boss meets his maker, the business that the employees have given their life to won't last long enough to ensure their own future.

A former student of mine once said to me after I noticed that he was no longer in my class, "Doc, I don't bitch, I just transfer." That's a great lesson. If employees are unwilling to accept the boss' plans for continuity, they should leave while there's enough time for them to do something in their own self interest.

Lenders should be concerned about what future security there is in their investment. *Customers* should worry because their sources could dry up. *Suppliers*, who are vitally interested in the perpetuation of their successful distributorships, ought to have a vital interest in the extended family as the source of successors--or of fatal conflict. If they don't, they could find themselves out of business in that territory. *Advisors* should understand and their actions should take into account their responsibility for the continuing success of their clients. I don't accept the attitude of some professionals who just shrug their shoulders at the demise of a client, as though they had no responsibility for his future. For my part, if I feel that my advice is ignored, that my clients are on a collision course with disaster because of their policies, I resign the account.

Everybody should take the time to give the business owner's business family the attention it deserves.

THE MULTIPLE HEIRS

Probably the biggest stake in having harmony among the extended family is held by the heirs. Our heirs are the good earth out of which the future is to grow and, therefore, they're probably the most important characters in this whole drama. As future successors, they have the greatest need to understand the world they inhabit, *a world that exists in all its complexity whether or not they actually decide to work in the business.* Their influence grows with the passage of time, particularly if they number more than one.

Not very often are businesses handed down to only sons of only sons. Usually there are multiple heirs and the potential ownership distribution gets very complex, as does the family management structure.

Many times, the expectations of the heirs far outstrip their ability, or the ability of the business, to handle or fulfill them. Even if the heirs decide not to come into the business, as long as they retain some ownership interest, their understanding and natural sense of entitlement and competitiveness with their brothers and sisters in the business can lead to a lot of harassment to the active family management.

This harassment can exhaust the working managers. I've seen it cause the dissolution of businesses, businesses which were otherwise successful.

If the business is going to succeed, there must be

successors, preferably successors who come out of the owning family(ies). Yet, in our seminars for young people, I've met and spoken to thousands of young sons and daughters of business owners and most of them have simply not been prepared, in any realistic way at all, to make *their* decision to join or not to join the business. In fact, more often they're systematically *mis*-trained...assuming they're even noticed.

THE SUDDENLY NOTICED KIDS

Sometime in his mid-forties, the founder usually realizes that his kids have become economic beings, something he probably first discovered the day his kids came to him for a job. At that point he was probably already tired of paying exhorbitant hourly rates to migrant labor for what he considered to be substandard performance, and he said to himself, "Hell, my kid can do that. Why give somebody else the money?"

As a clincher, he also realized that he could get even with the IRS by making his kids' allowances deductible, purely by allowing them wages and paying them with a company check. This even beats letting them use the company car for a date.

So the first job that the son or daughter has at the office or in the plant is usually on the same level as cutting the grass at home. It's *good* for the kid. It shapes him up.

This is all very convenient until "the kid" grows older and develops some serious economic interests. All of a sudden, the founder, who thought he had a 16-year-old messing around in the scrap pile, suddenly realized that the kid was the next generation in a potential dynasty.

His heirs enter their twenties, already having wondered for a number of years what they are going to do with their lives. Suddenly, Dad begins to realize that he has spawned something. It's no longer just a matter of survival. He's no longer just after security or status. He now begins to realize that what he's founded will have to be transferred to somebody else.

He has entered the foothills of the transition, and these hills get steeper and steeper as the years go by. He usually has more than one child, and they emerge consecutively, in two different sexes, and as persons with a future. The same is happening with his partner's children, if he has partners. They all have futures. Their parents want them to have futures. The kids want to have futures.

And, of course, there's this successful business with which something has to be done.

The founder feels a sense of urgency grow as the years pass and he gets less and less excited about the prospect of more hard work. This makes him more and more interested in his heirs as successors. The trouble is, his interest is too often more theoretical and philosophical than real. He knows he should give up the reins, but somehow the time never seems right.

THE RESTLESS SUCCESSOR

In some senses, the job the founder's successors face is tougher than what the founder had to do to start his business, but usually neither the founder nor his successors realize this.

The business was started because of Dad's independent nature and the fact that he couldn't really work for anybody else. So he blazed his new trail by himself. Because he didn't have an overseer or a boss, his mistakes went essentially unnoticed and uncriticized. His sole judge was the market and the market happened to like whatever he did that was right. Even the market didn't see too many of his mistakes.

Dad's successor is an entrepreneur in training. He's expected to become the trail blazer when Dad passes on his machete. He's expected to be independent, yet he is forced to work for one of the most domineering bosses in existence, a successful business owner. To make it worse, this "boss" is also the successor's father.

It's difficult. in general, for a student to know the time

when he should stop being a student and become a doer in his own right. Much has been written about the importance of having a mentor to guide one's professional development, a teacher whom the student respects and admires. Not too much has been said, however, about the process of weaning the student from the influence of the teacher.

It's over this precise issue that perhaps the most restlessness occurs among the key members of the business *mishpocheh* , the successors. The difficulty lies in knowing the difference between *teaching* and *telling* on the part of the teacher, as well as between *learning* and *imitating* on the part of the student.

For the founder, the duty to teach his successors increases with every passing year, but that duty doesn't necessarily bring with it the *ability* to teach well. A true teacher plants seeds in what he hopes is fertile soil, seeds which then sprout and grow in their own way with only as much of his help as is absolutely necessary.

The business founder, however, is by nature and tendency a gardener rather than a farmer. He plants seeds, but then he continues to prune, shape, cut, bend and generally do everything he can to make sure that what he has planted comes up precisely the way he wants it to be. It's what he's done with his business. It's what he's done with his managers. He usually tries to do it with his successor.

And believe me, this can cause the successor a lot of pain. He knows he's going to have to be tough and able to stand his own ground in a hostile environment when he takes over as president. So he has to be his own person. Yet his training is constantly pushing him in the direction of being fitted into his father's overall scheme like a rose on a trellis.

(Again let me remind you, it's the English language that makes it so convenient to keep referring to successors in the male gender. I'm sure you realize by now that I refer to both men *and* women when I say he, him and his.)

THE CRIME OF INEXPERIENCE

The poor kid comes into this situation almost defenseless, in most cases. Unfortunately, he usually hasn't worked for anyone else. He is untried, inexperienced, and poorly accepted by the people who surround and respect his father. There's little for him to do under these trying circumstances other than to imitate his teacher.

The successor doesn't have enough sophistication even to be able to tell good from bad. All he knows is that his father is a powerful, successful figure whom everybody seems to respect. So he concludes his father's way must be the best way. Dad, of course, believes the same thing and encourages this imitation.

If this student/successor is worth his salary, however, as time goes on his own personality begins to emerge, ever stronger and stronger. He begins to wrestle with a very fundamental conflict--whether or not to accept his own ideas over his father's.

Dad really didn't face this kind of question as he was building his business. He just had to make the lonely and frightening decisions about what to do. The successor may not be facing quite that much loneliness, but his decisions are complicated by the power of the teacher who raised him.

THE DILEMMA OF INDEPENDENCE

Would Dad agree with this decision? That question keeps coming up. Even though the successor may be almost certain that his father's opinion would be wrong, he faces the fact that what his boss does seems to work very well. He faces his love and respect for his Dad, all in addition to his fear of failing to make the right choice.

He's facing a dilemma of independence. On one side is his respect and gratitude. On the other is his need to assert his own (we hope) increasingly competent ideas and prove them (and himself) to himself and to his wife who probably thinks the same way he does.

This kind of pressure can lead either to open rebellion or to abject dependency. It has ruined many carefully thought out succession plans.

Then, as if the successor's problems weren't enough, into the business enter son #2, daughter #3 and, possibly, son-in-law #4--each feeling the need for self-expression. They each are faced, not only with Old Dad's dominance, but also their rivalry with each other, as it dawns on them that hierarchies usually only have one leader.

Mothers, of course, don't agree with the "one leader" concept, preferring instead a council of authority to replace Dad--and unconsciously to maintain her matriarchy. This usually ends up as a "family board" which effectively replaces any attempts at leadership with "group self-interest." Or, as a "novel idea," mothers often propose rotating presidencies.

It should be apparent that Mom's influence is going to be felt by Dad during this crucial stage, and it surely would be a sign of wisdom and common sense to have Mom and Dad in agreement.

I divide the responsibility here among the founder, Mom, and the successor(s) to see that the necessary teaching/learning process works. The teacher has the responsibility to allow the student growing room, giving encouragement and help rather than criticism and commands.

The student, on the other hand, needs more courage and self-confidence than we should ask of a normal human being. He must realize that if he fails to assert himself and use his own powers in his own ways at the right time, he will not be able to fill those considerable shoes.

THE INSTANT FAMILY

But even if we assume our own children have been properly provided for and get along well, it's important to remember that they usually don't live alone forever. Sons marry daughters-in-law, for example, and once they do, that young woman acquires an influence over her husband which is more powerful and more pervasive than any his parents could ever hope to have. Yet she's seldom given the due her potential power rates.

When she joins the family, she's an outsider, uncomfortable about her role and ignorant of her husband's work. If she is neglected by the rest of the family, as she often is, she usually has little option other than to become a determined enemy.

She will fight to defend and support only what she loves and understands. If she loves her husband but misunderstands the business, the resulting fireworks could snuff out a blast furnace.

Then, of course, there's the son-in-law, poor fella. If he happens to come to work in the business, he's tolerated only because he's the gorilla who's sleeping with the founder's baby. He's condemned because of a mistake he couldn't help--loving the founder's daughter.

The son-in-law has power even if he doesn't work in the business, because he married a shareholder-daughter. She *may* understand that she's expected to stay out of things and trust the working family members, or she may not--and in this day and age I count daughters-in-law as equal members--but it's a safe bet that the gorilla will have different ideas, particularly if he has some knowledge of business.

Obviously, we can't control the destiny of our children by picking out their spouses. Those days are gone, thank goodness. But what we *can* do is (1) raise our children well and (2) devote our efforts so that their spouses *will* understand us and our value systems and, hopefully, to accept us and what we do in our sense of fairness, just as we have to accept them.

This doesn't happen automatically. As soon as they are carried (or do the carrying) across the threshold of our immediate family, they should actively be brought into the family. It is essential that they know our dreams and understand what the founder and the rest of the members of the family are doing and why. They should know who fits where...and why. They must know they are welcome and that their concerns are as important as anybody's.

A FATAL EXAMPLE

I know of a manufacturing firm in the East, founded and built by a competent engineer. There are three sons, all married. The oldest--and most capable son has long been "groomed" for the presidency. The younger two boys just "haven't had enough experience."

The other day the founder called me and said his oldest son announced he's going to be leaving the family company to start his own business. I wasn't particularly surprised, knowing that this young man loved his wife and she'd been after him to get out of his father's business for a long time.

She's a fine person. I know her well. But she'd always been left out of family decisions. Her father-in-law strongly believed a wife's place is in the home, and because she's a nurse and had chosen to work, she took his general attitude to mean that he rejected her.

He *does* reject her, though unconsciously. She's not of his generation. She's not the girl he would have married. Often he doesn't agree with her attitudes or approaches. Because of his own confident and authoritarian personality, he throws these little barbs at her about her habits; the fact, for example, that her kids-- his grandchildren--spend "too much" time in day care.

She, in turn, doesn't understand *him*. Unlike her husband,

this woman hasn't known Dad all her life and has no built-in reason to be tolerant of his idiosyncracies. She also comes from a family that didn't own a business. Her father was an electronics technician for a major manufacturing company and he worked regular hours. He got vacations. He got overtime pay. All of this, of course, is unheard of for family members of a family-owned business.

Her husband, this founder's oldest son and presumed successor, was expected to work 12 to 14 hour days, always Saturdays, sometimes seven days a week--his father did at his age. He also had the usual conflicts with his father, conflicts which his father almost invariably won. But his wife, though she was a loyal and loving woman, wasn't ready to accept what she didn't understand.

It was never explained to her why her husband had to work so hard. Since her father-in-law seldom spoke to her as an equal, she had no way of understanding his motives or what he was trying to do.

This situation deteriorated to the point that the founder's oldest son, caught in the middle of a silent conflict he could do little to settle because of his dual loyalties, just threw in the towel in frustration.

I'm sure that nobody in that situation really understands what went wrong, but the gap between the founder and his son's wife is now so wide that it is almost unbridgeable. It's turned into a no-win situation and a very profitable business is going to suffer for years because of it, to say nothing of the family, the grandchildren, and the lives of his younger sons--now that his eldest has "deserted him." Let's hope Dad doesn't make the same mistakes again and again.

There are cases, of course, where there's been no hope from the beginning, or circumstances beyond our control take over.

Young men and women have been known to exercise colossally bad judgment in picking a mate. Sons in their mid-twenties, for example, have been known to go off and marry demanding 40-year-old divorcees with four children from two previous marriages. That has happened. It will happen again.

Or maybe a son and his new wife both happen to like the outdoor life and jump at a chance to move off to the mountains far away; or maybe the daughter takes over the business, and later her husband has an offer of an unexpected but spectacular promotion out of town. What *do* you do with an immobile business--and an ambitious young husband with ideas of a career of his own?

These circumstances don't happen every day, thank goodness. But when everyone climbs into that common bed known as "Die Firma," these crises will have to be faced over and over again. They simply can't be ignored--and lack of sincere communication among all partners is a signal that they will probably be mishandled.

It's because of the powerful and pervasive influence the extended family has on the future of the business that I recommend so strongly that great care be taken in raising our children (1) to understand wealth and its responsibilities, (2) not to be greedy, and (3) to be able to understand and accommodate the needs of *all* the family, young and old.

Partners, if the founder has them, usually also have children who aren't about to be disenfranchised when it comes time to distribute the stock and the management positions. That means that the business "cousins" will have to be able to work well together. They will have to understand each other. They will have to place the needs and requirements of the business in perspective with their individual differences.

Without active encouragement from their parents and later their spouses--the business "sisters-in-law"--they aren't likely to work this out themselves. In this context, I dare you to convince me of the innocence of those cheap shots about the partner's family--the other family--at the dinner table in front of our kids when they were little. Since we are all human, these errors are too often made--not in malice, usually--just thoughtlessly, out of envy for a difference in priorities or opportunities.

Just think about family A going on an expensive vacation (they only have 2 kids) while family B has to settle for a week in the state park with 5 kids. It's hard to be charitable when you're broke. The wounds can fester a long time, and it's a rare partnership that can survive the stings and barbs of envy.

THE NEED FOR A FAMILY CHART

You cannot draw an organization chart today in the family business without including a family chart. All shareholder interests, present *and* contemplated, must be considered and understood, along with an understanding of how the ownership division has evolved. Who is included and who is excluded--and why?

Unless these extended, enmeshed, and tangled relationships are considered and understood, and the economic consequences weighed, judged, and accepted, the family business is not understood. This road to understanding must be taken, not only by outsiders wishing to deal with a family business, but by the family as well. Without this understanding, events and decisions within that business will seem almost unintelligible.

An understanding of this extended family is absolutely crucial. The cast may be small in the beginning--a spouse, a few kids, a key man or two, a couple of advisors, and maybe Aunt Maude, who put up the money. Maybe there's a partner, too, who also has a spouse, and kids. But everything changes with time and success.

Say the partner's wife dies and he remarries a widow with two children of her own or, the founder's wife decides to get active in the business, or Aunt Maude dies and leaves her shares of stock to a charity managed by a trust from out of town. Or the key man says he'll quit if the kids come into the business, or the advisors tend to have less and less time for their old client--at least they're always out when he calls.

DRAW YOUR OWN CHART!
A PARTIAL CHECKLIST
OF THE EXTENDED BUSINESS FAMILY
(INCLUDE YOUR OWN MEMBERS AS APPROPRIATE!)

WHO THEY ARE & RANK IN ORDER OF THEIR IMPORTANCE TO YOU.	WHAT FACTORS CAN AFFECT THEIR INVOLVEMENT NOW OR LATER.....
YOU & YOUR SPOUSE	THEIR AGE(S).....
YOUR PARENTS AND GRANDPARENTS	THEIR HEALTH.....
	THEIR OCCUPATION.....
YOUR UNCLES & AUNTS	THEIR EDUCATION.....
YOUR SISTERS, BROTHERS AND COUSINS	THEIR MARITAL STATUS...
	THEIR SOURCE(S) OF INCOME.
YOUR SONS AND DAUGHTERS	THEIR INTELLIGENCE.....
	THEIR MOTIVATION.....
YOUR GRANDCHILDREN	THEIR EMOTIONAL STABILITY.....
AND ALL THEIR WIVES & HUSBANDS	THEIR OUTSIDE INTERESTS...
AND ALL THEIR KIDS & THEIR KIDS' MATES	THEIR TEMPERAMENTS.....
	THEIR COMPETENCE.....
	THEIR AMBITION.....
	THEIR PLANS FOR THEMSELVES.....

& DON'T FORGET TO ADD
PARTNERS.....
INVESTORS.....
MINORITY SHAREHOLDERS.....
KEY MANAGERS.....
& THEIR FAMILIES!

IT DOES GET INVOLVED - BUT REMEMBER
THE SIMPLER , THE BETTER.
(BUT NOT IF "SIMPLE" MEANS OVERLOOKED!)

LET IT ALL SHOW ON THE CHART
AND PLAN IN ACCORDANCE !

In addition to this, the son finds a mate, the daughter finds a mate, too, and though maybe neither is necessarily a person the founder would pick, still, they love each other, and the founder decides to be "fair" and takes everybody into the business.

With these changes and additions to this instant family, the class gets crowded--the teacher gets harassed and everything becomes all that much more complicated. The business owner and his spouse will find that it is absolutely necessary to take the young son-in-law (the "gorilla" who's sleeping with their baby), or the daughter-in-law ("that woman" who married their son and who now plays the role of "Tarantula"), and bring them all up to an acceptable understanding of the business.

No matter how good a job we've done with our own children, we cannot assume someone else did the same with our "instant" family. They were not raised to marry into our family and its business--it's enough to be able to rejoice that they love each other.

All we can really ask of God is that our children find decent, honest spouses. Instant family don't have to be CPA's or have degrees in chemical engineering. All we can ask is that they be nice kids, whose parents have raised them the best way they could. But, however they were raised, we will get the result.

The expanded business family is much larger than that family group that shows up at Christmas, weddings, wakes or *bar mitzvahs* . Instant family is increased by partners and investors, and *their* estate plans. It includes those non-family shareholders who are the fruit of grandpa's irresistable tendency to pass out small blocks of shares to everybody, because he wanted to be known as a nice guy or because he thought that would "motivate" them or because he was too stingy to pay in cash (...and forgot to make the stock offering "restrictive."), along with *their* mates and *their* children.

The world of people who are second-guessing the business owner becomes very, very large indeed. He's not just looking at them--they're also looking at him. As time passes without the necessary teaching being done, major gaps in understanding can develop, gaps which result almost inevitably in conflicting viewpoints. What the business owner sees as security in his old age, others will see as greed. What he considers to be his responsibility to the business, they will refer to as masochism or paranoia; what he sees as necessary, others will see either as neurosis, or as being in conflict with their own best self interest.

Restlessness within the business mishpocheh can either be a sign of an overwhelming desire to take charge and do what needs doing, or it can be a symptom of dissatisfaction and frustration.

Which it is for the business owner's expanding family will depend a lot on what has been done to prepare for and handle this facet of success.

Come with me to Macedonia and fight

"Commanders should be counseled chiefly by persons of known talent; by those who have made the art of war their particular study, and whose knowledge is derived from experience; by those who are present at the scene of action, who see the enemy, who see the advantages that occasions offer, and who, like people embarked on the same ship, are sharers of the danger. If, therefore, anyone thinks himself qualified to give advice respecting the war which I am to conduct, let him not refuse assistance to the state ... but come with me to Macedonia.

"He shall be furnished with a ship, a horse, a tent; even his traveling charges shall be defrayed. But if he thinks this too much trouble and prefers the repose of the city life to the toils of war, let him not on land assume the office of pilot.

"The city in itself furnishes an abundance of topics for conversation; let it confine its passion for talking to its own precincts and rest assured that we shall pay no attention to any counsel but such as shall be framed within our camp."

> LUCIUS AEMILIUS PAULUS
> Roman Consul
> Rome, 168 B. C.

THIS HISTORIC QUOTATION HUNG FOR YEARS IN THE PRIVATE OFFICE OF GENERAL OF THE ARMY DOUGLAS MacARTHUR, SUPREME COMMANDER ALLIED POWERS, AT HIS GENERAL HEADQUARTERS IN THE DAI ICHI BUILDING, TOKYO

Chapter 7

Recasting the One-Man Show

The founder built the business "ad hoc." It was put together by a committee of circumstances to emphasize his strengths. Usually, Dad is the management. Often, he's the principle product. Almost invariably, without him there'd be no business. The advisors were picked by him. The employees were hired by him. Into this set of clothes have to step the successors. It's a massive job.

Although we see the generations as forming a repeating circle, the business is at the same time forming an increasing spiral which can be called "more"--more opportunity, more problems, more resources, more everything. It is growing, and because of that growth, the successors to the business must begin their doing phase with more understanding than their predecessors, simply because there are more demands on their understanding.

The owner-manager's curve of "learn," "do," "teach," and "let go" is going to repeat, but with every generation, it will repeat at a higher level. It will repeat with five locations instead of one, or $5 million rather than 5,000 bucks, or 50 employees or 500 instead of three or 30.

Age and success have become partners, bringing demands that weren't there in the one-machine, one-shovel, one-store, one-product days. However it changed, the management problem will have accelerated and vastly increased the level of skill and understanding necessary to handle the business. With the increase also comes the possibility of accomplishing more with the business. This is what Dad is going to leave to his heirs, to his successors--the opportunity to do more and to do it better.

But often the result of the successor's desire to do even more with the family business ends up as a conflict between father and son. Ol' Dad appears to function to his successors as a constant obstacle to progress.

PREPARING FOR A NEW WORLD

Dad's memory is his worst enemy. Thirty years ago it was valid, but the world has changed. He still wants to keep doing. He's been doing damn well so far and he wants to keep doing and enjoying. The dreams, in short, begin to compete. Sons and heirs on the other hand have to realize that it was Dad's intuitive good sense that created the vehicle in the first place and must find ways to use this gift for the contributions it can make.

This is where it becomes absolutely crucial for Dad to understand that to stop doing is not to fade away and die. It is to begin *teaching*, to begin allowing his children to *do* with his help while he gives his example, his knowledge, and his love of the business to his now very extended business family. They, in turn, must understand the necessity of solving Dad's problems *before* they can begin to solve their own.

For example, in our seminars for young executives in the family business, we pass out little buttons with the letters "SDPF" (solve Dad's problems first), which are meant to emphasize the fact that successors should never be part of the problem, only a source of their solution.

The key is to help Dad solve *his* problems and he'll be more than glad to give more and more of them away. His big fear is that his successors won't understand. *Confidence* in the commitment and contribution of his heirs may be the greatest gift we give to business fathers.

None of this is easy, as every business family discovers in its own time. Dad's generally not a good teacher. He's a doer. He's not articulate. He explains very little. When he gets stuck, he grunts and the kids are supposed to say "yes" so the old man doesn't think they're stupid. It's a hell of a way to run a class.

Even if Dad is a good teacher, it's not enough. The son can't learn if he doesn't put in the effort--and, even with effort, he can't afford to learn only what his father has to teach. The world is getting more and more complex, and needs are accelerating at a faster rate. This is no longer a world in which multiple generations of bricklayers can build a cathedral--the grandson laying brick for the third story on top of brick his father laid on the second story, on top of grandpa's ground floor.

Not even a graduate education is enough by itself to enable a successor successfully to operate a family business. A formal education may take care of the technical knowledge that Dad might lack about the increased complexities of the outside world--an MBA, for example, is usually enough for General Motors or Standard Oil, because they mostly deal with technical problems in an increasingly technological society--but in a family business things are not so simple as the complexities of management techniques. Because of this, decisions must be made, and they must be made as early as possible.

THE AGING MALE

During the years when the urgency of acceleration is removed and the founder is starting to sit more lightly in his seat, he flies into a point of decision. He must decide whether the business he built is going to make it for another generation.

This question becomes more pressing as the years pass and usually its answer becomes less, rather than more, certain. So much is taken for granted in the beginning of the business. So much more isn't even thought about. But as time passes, the major concerns become more and more insistent, and the problems less and less solvable.

The hairy-chested hero inevitably becomes the aging male. His wife becomes a referee/acrobat, maintaining peace in the family while juggling her loyalty to her husband, her love for her children, and her justifiable concern for her own security. She looks at her overworked husband and begins to think that she may be a widow in waiting.

Her husband is getting tired of discipline, the discipline of getting up every morning and going to the shop, going to the marketplace, meeting the union, meeting the payroll, meeting the creditors, and meeting deadlines. He's so tired that he has become a very undisciplined guy in his personal life. He doesn't want to be disciplined anymore.

He's sick of taking it out on himself, of denying himself and of draining his willpower. This is why self-development is so hard for the owner-manager. This is why he tends to drink too much or act in various other excessive ways. It's his way of maintaining stability in the face of exhaustion.

He has always made the big, important decisions. Everybody delegates upward to him. No matter what the problems are, *he* has to solve them--whether it's the color of the letterhead, the hours for lunch, whose vacation takes precedence over whose, or the million other items of trivia which are delegated to Him because it's His business, His money, and He's

The Boss.

This is why there's so much opportunity for leadership in volunteer associations and other such environments. In the majority of these cases the business owner is ready to follow on any subject which doesn't much concern him.

Where do you want to go to lunch? Upstairs, downstairs--he doesn't much care. He'll follow. In associations and other environments where this big hero can find someone else willing to lead, he wants to be the willing follower.

I realize this isn't always true. Sometimes the divinity with which the business owner endows his business decisions leads him to the sad conclusions that only he can do or decide anything. But these guys usually die young.

He's exhausted. He'd just like to keep what he has, Lord. He doesn't need any more. He just wants to protect and nuture his possessions and carry them off with him into some permanent sunset.

THE READY RETIREE?

To the uninitiated, all this would imply that our successful founder is just waiting for somebody to take his business off his hands.

On the surface this is what it *does* look like. It's even what he says. But there's one major obstacle. For a business to prepetuate it has to change and grow, which he knows means anything but a release from the pressure he's under. It means more risk and more damn hard work. The whole idea seems almost obscene.

Growth can be defined in many ways, but by most definitions, a business can't survive without it. In its best sense, growth offers an increasing opportunity to do meaningful work to those who are involved in the business. It also offers that opportunity to the people who must be attracted and retained in order to continue it.

Growth isn't just a function of economic size. It is a function of how satisfied people are with themselves and their work. Economic growth is necessary, however, to maintain market share and economic power, but this growth is also necessary for maintaining *organizational* power.

Consider, for example, the problem of the successful 60-year-old founder with 40-year-old managers whom he wants to stay around while his 25-year-old sons are growing up. He'd better make sure he has expanding jobs for those managers to fill for 20 years.

If he has six kids and he'd really like them all in the business, he'd better make sure that the business will be large enough to absorb them when the time comes. If he wants to have a comfortable, secure retirement, he'd better make sure that there's enough of a going concern left behind after he leaves to support his wishes.

This means that there will always be a need for that "little bit more," because the business has to grow or there's no future for it. It has to change, too. The one-man show has to be redesigned to accommodate a new cast--and that's anything but a cinch.

The old star isn't going to be all that ready to move off of center stage out of the spotlight. He may *want* to, but his life has been absorbed with little more than preparing for and relishing the starring role, and to learn to do something else can be a monumental task.

The business was designed, almost by accident, over the years to fit the founder like a glove. The part was written for him. The supporting cast was chosen because they worked well with him. There's hardly a successor in the world who could succeed him in *his* role, so a new role must be provided. It must grow out of the growth of the business.

THE SUCCESSOR CAN'T BE AN UNDERSTUDY

The successor can't just be an understudy to the founder. In that role, he would only imitate, badly, what someone else learned over many years to do well. It's more accurate to think of the successor as a professional manager in apprenticeship. He's learning to run a business in a changing and increasingly complex world.

Imitation won't do it. Only knowledge, wisdom, experience and good judgment will. The successor has to forge his own world or he is likely to fail.

This means that he can't expect to succeed if he inherits a business built solidly and solely around his Dad. He can't assume that all he has to do is to do what Dad did, because that's not enough.

To ignore change is to plan about as effectively as the French army in the early days of World War II. The French expected that wars would be fought as the First World War was fought 25 years before, and, as every history student now knows, they were completely overwhelmed by new strategy in only nine months.

Dad created the business to use his own talents and abilities in a world that accepted and used them. But today's world is characterized by an accelerated rate of change. What worked in the past may no longer be applicable. Products, markets, and technologies change and the organizations dealing with them intermix differently.

The successor must inherit and contribute to a plan that will meet the future needs of the company. Too often, unfortunately, this is exactly what he does not inherit. What he gets are dubious markets and products and technologies from the past, along with all the malcontents and back-whollopers the founder picked up because Dad was hiring on the come in the early years.

Even after 20 years of successful operation, there are too

few people on most management teams with maturity, ability, and some demonstrated potential for future leadership. The key managers in a successful founder-managed company are usually the boss's contemporaries, people who tend to believe that if they can hold on as long as the boss, they're all set. If he quits at 65, they're ready to quit too, but if he hangs on--so can they.

Needless to say, there is not a lot of encouragement from these old-timers to bolster the successor's career. To many of them, his graduation to general management would signal catastrophe, so they do what any of us would do under these circumstances. They damn him with faint praise. "He's really coming along, J.B." "Just a couple more years, Chief, and I think we'll have ourselves a good boy."

These smart old politicians also are careful to remind the boss constantly of the past glories of the good old days; glories, of course, in which they all took part.

Naturally, under these conditions they worry a lot about what might happen if the boss suddenly left the scene. As long as he doesn't change the rules on them, they view him as security. This is why they worry about that day when "the kids take over."

BAREFOOT AND PREGNANT

These long term employees also realize at some point in their career, usually some time in their late 40's, that they are essentially unemployable elsewhere. There's no way that a man with 15 or 20 years in a family company is going to become a responsible manager of a public company. It might happen earlier, at 25 or 30, but certainly not beyond that. The progression is usually from public to private, not the other way around.

Most managers didn't realize how finally and irrevocably their futures were being set when they went to work for the founder.

Some employees accepted their original, marginal,

low-pay job because they never were any good, and now they're being kept on as overclassed serfs. Others may have gotten so many "circumstantial" pay raises that they've long been priced out of any reasonably competitive job market. They get used to living their way and they want to keep it.

If there's one question that keeps coming up at our seminars it's the successor's question about what to do with the "old guard" Dad left behind. There's no easy answer. If they are left behind, the successor faces a heartbreaking, draining task. Good advice is hard to give...and even harder to accept.

I'm reminded of a quotation which Douglas MacArthur kept in his office:

> *"Commanders should be counseled chiefly by persons of known talent; by those who have made the art of war their particular study, and whose knowledge is derived from experience; by those who are present at the scene of action, who see the enemy, who see the advantages that occasions offer, and who, like people embarked on the same ship, are sharers of the danger. If, therefore, anyone thinks himself qualified to give advice respecting the war which I am to conduct, let him not refuse assistance to the state...but come with me to Macedonia.*
>
> *"He shall be furnished with a ship, a horse, a tent; even his traveling charges shall be defrayed. But if he thinks this too much trouble and prefers the repose of the city life to the toils of war, let him not on land assume the office of pilot.*
>
> *"The city in itself furnishes an abundance of topics for conversation; let it confine its passion for talking to its own precincts and rest assured that we shall pay no attention to any counsel but such as shall be framed within our camp.* (Lucius Aemilius Paulus, Roman Consul, Rome, 168 B.C.)"

THE BOSS SHOULD CLEAR THE DEADWOOD

It shouldn't be the successor's job. It's the founder's responsibility to look at his management team and ask himself how well he's done the job of making sure they are equipped and available for the future. Which does he have, managers or high class technicians and mechanics? If his key people don't think and act like managers and executives, they are not a management team. They are overpaid tradesmen--and possibly overdue for any significant role in the future.

This doesn't often happen in public companies because they *expect* leadership from their management. I know this isn't always true (cf. Chrysler, Penn Central, Lockheed), but in theory that is what their boards were supposed to be considering. In privately owned companies, however, it's not even a theory. Management leadership is not even considered to be a responsibility of the board--and the results show.

In the vast majority of public corporations, managers are trained, they are given responsibility, and they evolve into a special breed of executive. Professional managers in public companies may or may not be paid as much as some key people in closely held companies, but they are surely more sophisticated. In the family-owned company, too often the boss himself has a hard time becoming--or staying--sophisticated, without worrying about the development needs of his illiterate managers. (There is very little difference in my mind between people who can't read and people who won't read.)

This is why it's so important for the founder to think about--and to do something about--the growth of his managers as early as possible. If he fails to do this, the day will inevitably arrive when it's almost too late to do anything. Eventually, these managers become unemployable, and therefore, almost unfirable. Their resumes are too anemic to allow them to survive in the outside world.

It's unlikely, for example, that a 50-year-old sales manager for a $2 million company can leave and become a sales manager for a $50 million company. And it's no more realistic to expect him to go happily from being sales manager to being salesman, or from foreman to lathe operator. Not by his choice, anyway.

Not *if*, but *when* these people falter, they're not totally to blame. Consider what it's like to work for the founder. He's mean, he's irascible. He's tough, erratic, sometimes even a little brilliant. He's not the easiest person in the world to understand and follow. Even though his key people may be called managers, they don't have a lot of control, however, over their actions and environment.

These managers and employees, at least those who stick around for any significant length of time, become very dependent on the founder's future for *their* futures. This may be an uncomfortable thought, but it's generally true. Working in a family-owned business tends to become a terminal occupation after a certain period on the job.

IT'S THE FOUNDER'S RESPONSIBILITY

The founder hired this team. It's his responsibility to be concerned for their well-being, and to make sure they continue to grow on the job. The founder owes much of his past success to them.

But what the company needs for the future is a functioning, harmonious team that is adjusted to and accepts the idea of the founder's succession. (As the hopeful young boy said to the girl, "I don't want your tacit acquiesence--I would like your enthusiastic participation.") This is no easy task, but it is one that can best be done by Dad. I've seen too many businesses in which the old managers greet "the kid" either by resigning on the job, starting a mutiny, or doing everything they can to poison the young prince--or, increasingly, princess.

It's the Boss's duty to make sure that the managers he hired and trained don't suddenly become known as "they." Most managers aren't at the controls. The founder is. Their attitudes, to a great extent, depend upon what they're told, how it's told, how much they know, and how much they believe their Boss.

The Boss should honestly tell these employees and managers that his business is either going to be run by members of his family, or he's going to have to sell it, and most likely, they and the managers don't have enough money--individually or collectively--to buy it.

After knowing his family, if they can't be proud of them and willing to work with them, they should understand the boss would be glad to help any of them recreate their careers elsewhere. Their responsibility is clear. They have to help make his family the best management team they can create.

The boss's children, on the other hand, must realize the tremendous contribution these continuing employees make to their well-being, and should look forward to having this help available as long as these dedicated employees can serve.

The problem is even more complex in businesses with multiple owners. Too often managers in these companies find themselves forced to pick sides, guessing which of the business brothers or cousins is going to win or which of the partners will come out on top. Betting on the survivor of a buy/sell agreement becomes a sporting event where "winner takes all."

But it's devastating. The managers are in an airplane flying in a the dark and there's no way that the wrestling between the pilots isn't going to upset the passengers. It makes them want to get out at the next stop before they all get killed. For any potential successor, walking into a situation like this is like standing up in no-man's-land wearing an aloha shirt.

If the founder *needs* new managers, the sooner he gets them, the better off he will be. If he's *got* good people, then the sooner he solves their problems--e.g. the need for opportunity and fulfillment on the job, along with security, trust, and open communication--then the sooner they'll start solving his--e.g. the need for continuity, cooperation, and confidence in the future.

His managers will someday become "instant" employees

to his successors, and if they are predisposed to mistrust, dislike, or take pot shots at "the kids," neither they nor the kids will have much of a chance. Energetic managers have to be developed for the needs of the future. Deadwood must be pruned. Non-family managers and the family successors must learn to respect and accept each other for their specific contribution to the whole.

And all this has to be done in the founder's spare time while he fights off the competitors, placates the customers, argues with the suppliers, worries about the IRS, and hallucinates about his steadily receeding nirvana.

You see why he can't just sit back and enjoy it?

SURVIVAL IS THE GOAL

Founders, successors, and managers should have one major goal in common: *Perpetuating the business*. Each has his own responsibilities in making sure the goal is reached, but each must also work with the others and understand what's really needed.

Many of the succession plans I see are feats of technical wizardry. They're put together in the erotic dreams of financial planners, tax lawyers, and others. But, even with all their fascinating technicalities, they often don't go to the real guts of the problem of continuity.

There is a lot more involved here than just minimizing, avoiding or deferring taxation. All that does is increase the funds available to fuel the plan. But WHERE IS THE PLAN?

Plans have to be made to ensure that the *business actually survives*. This is the whole point and it is a matter of management.

THE IMPORTANT QUESTIONS

The survival of any business depends upon the continuing and competent attention of those involved. For the *founder*, this means asking himself questions, specific questions, about his business and the future:

1) Has he developed a real team of **competent managers** for the future...or is he hanging on with loyal, over-age incompetents?

2) Does his **accounting system** make his business understandable and clarify the decisions of his management...or does he use it solely to confuse the IRS? Is he the only one who knows what's going on?

3) Does his **family** really understand and share his goals, his hopes, his objectives, and his dreams...or do they all just feel entitled to get something out of him?

4) Are his **advisors** really the best he can find...qualified, committed, and working hard to assure the success of his plans...or are they inadequate co-conspirators doing him and the business more harm than good?

5) Is his **board** made up of capable, working outside directors...or is it a place to put relatives, obsolescent employees, and self-interested "friends"?

6) And finally, has he faced the fact that even though he may be divine, he's probably not immortal, and that unless he chooses, develops, and installs competent **successors** ...his executors will do it for him.

For the *successor* , the survival of the business requires experience, an understanding of business management. It requires constant work with the present management team, both to get a feel for what they can do as well as to gain their respect and confidence. *Entrepreneur* though he will be, he must also become a professional *manager* .

Because there are usually *multiple heirs* , sometimes to multiple owners in varying blood, legal,and marital relationships, there must also be trust and accommodation among the next generation of family managers. The founders, ideally with the help of an objective board of outside directors, will have to select the next president from a pool of their offspring/managers.

The next president must be one person. There's room for only one leader on a team, and all of the heirs--as well as

Momma--must understand and accept this fact. The managers, too, must realize they were happy before without being president--why change now?

The goal of everybody involved should be to transfer management and ownership in such a way as to prevent the all too common conflicts that can cripple or destroy a business. The survival of the business should be the major objective of everything that's done.

THE ONLY CRITERION: COMPETENCE

The yardstick for managerial selection and employment must be as practical and objective as possible--and the best one I know is the yardstick of *competence*. A business is too fragile and valuable to allow the passing out of management positions on the basis of blood alone, so the same judgments I'm suggesting the founder place on his managers, he should place upon his potential successor.

This demand for competence places a greater challenge on the successors, of course, but I have seen over and over again that it makes the management transition easier and less traumatic for all involved. This is why I'm so much in favor of all successors cutting their management teeth by *working for somebody else* until they have gained significant managerial judgment.

Under another's roof, the business owner's son or daughter is just another employee. They can learn to sink or sail depending on their own actions and their own abilities. They also have a chance to learn management from *professional managers*, discovering that there are other good ways to do things than just the way Dad does them, or the ways they dream up in their innocence.

To be specific, I'd choose an appropriate publicly held company in an allied field. After all, why can't our kids cut it on the same basis as others in an entry level job? They are free, educated, and 21. I'll guarantee that they'll learn more about business in five years in this environment than in the same 60 months working (?) for a subjective father who honestly doesn't have the experience for this responsibility.

We really shouldn't practice on our own--it's too traumatic. Remember what happened when you tried to teach your children to drive.

Clearly, there are some exceptions. For example, where the offspring has evidenced a desire since childhood to "work for Dad"--almost like a vocation in the priesthood, and probably as rare--but of the thousands of kids I've seen end up working for Old Dad right out of school, most do so because it's so much easier to con Dad or Mom than an outside recruiter for a professional company. It pays better, too, has lower standards of discipline, and the job security is tremendous--especially after the grandchildren arrive.

Don't think I'm being harsh--I've spoken to too many thousands of heirs of business owners at all ages. If they could do it over again, 85% would work outside the family business first, then bring their enthusiasm, talent, and experience to bear where it counts, when it counts, around the age of 30.

At this point, Dad is probably not much over 60 anyway and is *just beginning* to think about *thinking* about retiring. He doesn't need to have an over-motivated, under-qualified kid yapping at his heels five years sooner wondering when he's going to be delegated more responsibilities.

SOMEDAY, SON...

This period of outside experience can be crucial to a smooth succession. For example, a business owner I know very well has recently been honored by his community for his years of work in the arts, charity and public service. He's a multi-talented man with a warm and sharing personality. I feel honored to be his friend.

Yet, as I read the clipping his wife sent me which described accomplishment after accomplishment, I began thinking about his children, particularly the ones who are to be his successors in the business. They don't have a very easy job ahead of them. They are under pressure to imitate his strengths, without picking up his weaknesses. This is fundamentally unfair.

Dad's weaknesses are probably the opposite pole of his strengths--the way absent-mindedness tends to go along with genius. To expect only Dad's strengths to be imitated is like expecting a magnet to have only one pole. The successor's response is usually frustration.

This frustration takes many forms. Often the son or daughter expresses a disdain for the business, as though it really isn't important. Sometimes, in confusion and disappointment, they reject the business and their father's values as ridiculous--or maybe even destructive. Occasionally, they become "palace revolutionaries," seeking to overthrow and change what they can't comprehend.

A more passive, but equally common reaction can be a loss of drive or self-confidence. The seemingly unattainable become the factually impossible.

Stepping into someone else's shoes is as undesirable and as unlikely as sharing their skin. But this has to be explained, and nobody should be able to do it better than those of us who are their supposed "heroes."

The temptation is great to accept the applause of the world, to begin to believe in our own perfection. After this, the natural conclusion is that our kids could do no better than come up behind us as little carbon copies. It commonly happens, and it's usually destructive.

I remember a young man I met at one of our Young Executive Seminars a few years ago. He was telling me how impossible it was going to be to succeed his father. I tried to tell him that succession didn't mean matching what his father did, that it meant learning from his strengths and *building on those accomplishments* , but he kept shaking his head.

"Tell that to the world," he said to me. "Dad's made it, so everybody forgets his mistakes. I *haven't* made it, so I'm expected to do everything he does right, without excusing my mistakes."

This young man was becoming terminally awed by his father's reputation.

Reputation is a powerful thing, and it leads people to some very unusual conclusions about the person who has that reputation. A good example is a story told about Beethoven. One day, after the great composer--who was also a virtuoso--had played a concert, a woman came up to him and said, "Maestro, you are a genius! What a great gift to play like that."

"Madame," Beethoven is said to have replied, "If you practiced 12 hours a day for 40 years as I have, you, too, could be a 'genius.'"

Talent is only an enabler. *Competence* is the engine that gets things done, and it is developed only through sweat, mistakes, bruises, and frustration. Every Achilles has his heel, and who knows this better than us battle-scarred, graying old warriors? But do any of us take the time to tell our successors that we also see what they see in ourselves. Do we ever discuss our weaknesses, doubts, and frustrations as well as our strengths?

In order to succeed, our heirs must make their own way, as we have, but it would sure help them to know that even the most talented have a lot of scars and some pretty bad moves. The real pros know how to accept applause with perspective.

A great reputation may be handy for getting laurels from the public, but it has no place in the locker room, where only honesty among equals can ensure success for the team. The new quarterbacks learn from the old greats to develop their unique talent, and to suffer from an equally unique set of weaknesses.

This is a crucial lesson for our successors to learn, but one which is seldom taught.

Nepotism in its ideal form is the selection of blood kin for a good job out of a pool of equally qualified candidates. The nepot, under these circumstances, isn't being given a gift. He's getting an opportunity he's earned by the sweat of his brow, while his accident of birth is merely a happy advantage.

THE CLOSED SOCIETY

That's the ideal. The reason it doesn't happen that way in so many family-owned companies is *loneliness* . The business owner, his successors, his managers and his family tend to suffer from a very common problem: they inhabit a very small world.

As far as matters of business go, there is little, if any, meaningful interaction with outsiders on matters important to the transition. The thinking and all the activity tends to center on immediate concerns, sudden problems and petty disagreements. Value judgments, operating policies, and major assumptions are seldom questioned, much less changed.

But with success comes the growing need for the founder to start examining everything he takes for granted. By the time he's thinking about coasting out of his most productive years, he should already have begun sharing the problem with people whose opinion he accepts.

He doesn't need anything formal in the beginning. Maybe simply a meeting with people he knows and respects in a non-formal way. But the important thing is for the founder to become comfortable being interrogated. He should learn to feel comfortable preparing for a meeting of his peers.

Business owners generally don't like to be introspective or to meet and talk. They are doers, and meetings which make them sit back and think, ask, and prepare for, go against their basic grain. But as time goes by and the business grows, such meetings will become more and more necessary. Any attempt the founder can make at sharing the problems will help smooth the way for the more formal approach eventually needed for a successful transition of management.

The founder must learn to share his problems with his family and his managers. He must share them with his children and with his advisors as they develop. Even these informal meetings will start bringing to light some of the difficult questions that will have to be examined. This is the beginning of a periodic, but increasingly regular *audit* of all of the important questions about business management and continuity.

As a consultant for many years, I have always been shocked by so often being the first person that the business owner has ever leveled with. The people he has been around for years and years don't realize how they have failed him in not creating an atmosphere--a forum--for honest discussion, instead of hiding the valid concerns under a guise of meaningless small talk.

INSTALLING THE OUTSIDE BOARD

The sooner the founder learns to share his problems, the sooner he will get used to the cold shock of being questioned by an outsider, and the sooner he will be ready to take the necessary step of creating and installing a legally constituted body charged with ensuring the continuity and perpetuation of the business: a working board of outside directors, a group of committed, concerned, compassionate and courageous risk-taking peers of the owner-manager, who want to help him, have the experience to help, and would accept the opportunity as a challenge to them. (For a more detailed study of the outside board, reference can be made to *BEYOND SURVIVAL* pages 121 to 141.)

The business owner's managers and his advisors--his accountant, his banker, his attorney, and consultants of all types--are professional technicians. He needs them for his tactical planning and for facing the battles at hand. But directors are essentially *strategists* . Their subject is the total thrust of the business and where it's going.

Fundamental risk judgments should always be made by competent, experienced *risk-takers* --the kind of people who should be on the board of the successful family owned business, not Mom, Uncle Charlie, maybe a couple of the kids, and

Rasputin the advisor. I've always admired the stand of the A.I.C.P.A.-- (The American Institute of Certified Public Accountants)--who have long had the stated policy of prohibiting board memberships by any of their members where they are engaged in rendering professional advice to them as clients.

What the founder--and the business--need is the tested knowldge and experience of someone who is in the position to be able to confirm or challenge the *risk* judgments of the owner.

Paid advisors have knowledge, but rarely are they in the position to start challenging the owner's judgments openly. They work for him, after all. Their livelihood depends on his funds, his good will, and his continued blessing. Besides, the nature of their expertise and experience doesn't usually include the trade-offs and decisions of risk taking. They are analyzers, and recommenders--not generally decision makers--except by default.

Directors of a family-owned company, if they protect anybody, should protect the president from his own power. Clearly, whoever is going to act as a legitimate pressure group on the owner-manager must be someone who is capable of breaking through the founder's stubborn pride as well as of withstanding his onslaughts.

This is no easy role. It's one thing to give an owner-manager advice on, say, cash flow management or government regulation, and an entirely different thing to understand and help a man whose personal and corporate goals are all intertwined, whose personal limits are often the limits he imposes on the company, and whose age increasingly becomes a factor in his decision making.

The risk-taking peer has been through all that. He understands. And he's not about to be intimidated by the owner-manager's flak.

The outside director's help is absolutely necessary if the one man show the founder has built is to be successfully perpetuated in the next generation. He can help answer the serious questions in a way acceptable to all involved: the multiple owners, the managers and even the people outside the company. Such questions as these must be asked: Which of the available heirs should be the successor? Is it fair to make such a choice? Is it equitable? Who will judge the qualities and abilities of the potential heirs? Mother? Dad? What about the sequence of birth, the accident of sex, the pressure from a spouse? What if the heir doesn't want the job?

I've seen some sad cases where the owner-founder continually waits and assumes that his prodigal children are going to reform their ways and return to the fold to take up their dutiful management of the company. This may make a nice parable in the scriptures, but in business it tends to be a disastrous fantasy.

A board of risk-taking peers, assuming some collective continuity, can serve as a judging body, watching and evaluating both the potential successor and the succession plan. Even the choice of a competent successor presumes that the transfer of ownership will occur over a reasonable and adequate period of time. But there's nobody less objective about the time remaining, in general, than the business owner himself.

A working board of outside directors, because they can see through the smoke screens, can force the owner-manager to give due consideration to his succession years sooner than he would come to that decision on his own.

MUCH IS REQUIRED

The successful perpetuation of a family-owned business requires the founder's acceptance of the need for growth, his adaptation to the fact of change, and his preparation of his management team for the next generation. It requires an ability in the successor to build upon what his father has started, which is so much more than mere imitation. It requires, too, the judgment, understanding and objectivity of committed and compassionate overseers--the outside directors.

The formula for recasting the one-man-show isn't all that

complex. It's just that it requires dedication, confidence, and a willingness to be open to the ideas of others.

It also requires as early a start as possible.

Chapter 8

Giving It All Away

Perhaps the most critical question for continuity of any family business is what is done with the shares. In the beginning, the founders have it all. But then estate plans are put together--too often when they are lying awake in bed at three a.m. Common stock takes on the purple cloak of Dad's love, generosity, and even-handedness. When it's distributed without serious thought of consequence to working and non-working heirs alike, events are set in motion that are almost irreversible--and successful continuity is severely threatened.

The founder-architect builds his dream mostly to achieve his own goals, whatever they are--freedom, wealth, respect, power--and usually by the time he reaches the top of his curve he has achieved most of those goals.

But that's not usually enough, because goals don't stay static. They change and grow as the founder and his circumstances change. What the successfull business founder almost inevitably discovers--even with his earlier goals achieved and safely packed away in his personal safe--is that another goal comes to stand between him and a serene old age.

The successful founder has already gone from "doing" to "teaching." He's had to bequeath to others the knowledge, judgment and experience he's accumulated. But teaching isn't his only ultimate responsibility as he prepares himself, his family, and his business for the challenge and growth ahead. He has one further job: *He has to do something with the business,* because nobody's managed yet to take anything along when the lid is slammed on the box.

In our later years, we shuffle a lot of papers and exchange paper "A" for papers "B" or "C," but when it's all over, everything goes to somebody else in some measure--our cares, our abilities, and our dreams, as well as our funds.

YET ANOTHER SHIFT IN ROLES

The successful founder must somehow find the strength and the ability to shift his roles again with the further passage of time. He has to seek the wisdom to accept age as an increasingly influential partner, and he has to learn to listen to the subtle advice that his partner is trying to give.

Because he cannot take it with him, the founder must eventually begin the complex task of *giving it all away.* And he must do it in such a way as to generate acceptance among his family that what he has done is "fair." The agreement of his family on his concept of fairness is essential to the well-being of all.

There's more than just material wealth to be given away. We also have the responsibility to pass on a successful and functioning business. We have to give away what knowledge and understanding we have acquired to others, to people who can actually *do* something with that knowledge and understanding.

But we also have to give away the burdens we've carried on our shoulders almost by ourselves from the beginning, the burdens that come with wealth and responsibility.

The trouble the founder has, however, is that he's been alone with the challenge of running his business so long that he's accepted the problems and concerns as part of himself, and as a natural part of his life. He may admit that he has to give his *wealth* away, but the worries are something else entirely. They're *his*. Always have been. Nobody else could ever understand them as well as he can, he assumes, so they can't possibly be shared. This flawed logic has some disastrous corrolaries.

Since the problems are such an intimate part of running the business, instead of being able to plan carefully to transfer both his wealth and his problems to someone who's been prepared to accept and handle both, the founder is forced to hold on in desperation, hoping someday somebody else will understand his *troubles* enough so that someday he can really be free. But that person never seems to show up.

Never, that is, unless the founder has done something to make sure his business will continue through the efforts and abilities and dedication of his successors. This requires preparation.

The ability to accept wealth and responsibility isn't inbred in our children. To bring that ability into existence, we have to assume success from the beginning, teaching our children how to handle it and what it requires.

Once we actually do reach the point of success, our heirs stand before us as they are. We have done our best and they are ready or not ready as the fates may have it. As discussed earlier, there are a number of actions we can take along the way to our children's maturity to help tip the scale in favor of communication within the family.

Here, however, I have no alternative but to assume that

the *successful* founder has been fortunate and is blessed with heirs and potential successors who understand the heritage of wealth and who are ready for the challenges, responsibilities, and demands the family business will bring to them. If the founder has not filled these prerequisites, the chances that he will be able to see his dream successfully perpetuated among his heirs are very, very slim.

At our seminars for young family business successors, both those heirs now working full time in the business and those young people who aren't quite sure what they want to do about the business, I find that they have very set ideas about their role. If their ideas are positive, usually they've been created by a conscious effort on the part of concerned and communicative parents. Where those attitudes are negative, they've more often than not been reinforced by "outside influences"--classmates, friends, neighbors, teachers, etc.

Often these people have seized upon all sorts of incidents they know about, all designed to make inheritors feel uncomfortable in their position of privilege. As a reaction, heirs often become anti-social in their appearance and actions. These attitudes can be changed, but it would sure be less complicated if done right the first time.

Parents who are business owners deserve an equal voice in presenting what they hold to be true and important to their own children. Unfortunately, not too many of us take the time along the way to do this, and we're always upset when the views held by our children are not in keeping with ours.

TRANSFER WITHOUT CONFLICT

But, even assuming that the business can be perpetuated and the founder's wealth can be safely distributed among good kids, some major questions still exist. The founder has to determine *what* he shall give to whom and in what form.

Most business founders have multiple children of both

sexes. They usually have varied degrees of interest and experience. Each is a little bit different in talent and needs, and this is why "giving it all away" comes in infinite variations, depending on the specific facts. Every founder, when deciding how to give it all away, has to consider the facts of his wife, his multiple children, his multiple partners, their multiple children and wives, as well as whole groups of interested people--other minority owners, employees past and present, even creditors can become involved.

The survival and growth of the founder's company depends to a very great extent upon how wisely and humanely management and ownership has been transferred. The founder's goal should be to transfer management and ownership in such a way as to make sure that he prevents the conflicts that have crippled and destroyed so many businesses.

He may even have to face the further question of whether or not the family and the management should really be the same thing. Continued family control may or may not be an asset to the business, but few founders seem able to take realistic looks at the business abilities of various family members.

It's relatively common to measure family managers against non-family key employees, of course. That's done all the time. But this comparison usually does more harm than good because it's just not done objectively. Either the kid is no damn good or he can do no wrong. There's no middle ground.

As I said before, *competence* and *commitment* must be major yardsticks, because the business is too fragile and valuable to be passed out on any other basis. And competence of family members who want to be family business managers is best judged by outsiders.

These judgments can come from people outside of the business who have employed the heirs. These judgments can come from objective directors who have no axe to grind other than the successful perpetuation of the business. Such judgments seldom can be made with any real objectivity and accuracy by the founder or other members of the owning family, or by the employees who themselves are going to be affected in that position.

It would appear obvious then that the better known and the longer known and the more precisely evaluated the successor can be to those making these judgments, the more likely it is that we as parents can accept such views as valid and not dismiss them out of hand with statements such as, "Well they really haven't known George (or Mary) as we have."

Yet how often do we create such an atmosphere in which our children can be measured? Very seldom. It's almost as though we were fearful of the results, a little like dictators who perpetually postpone the elections until the crisis is over--which it never is. Usually, the elections are too late--both for dictators and for businesses.

THE PROBLEM OF EQUITY DISTRIBUTION

The same sort of consideration must go into the matter of equity distribution. Who, in fact, should get the marbles? And in what form? Why? These are invariably extremely agonizing questions for many owner-managers and for their spouses. They tend to think of the business as a heritage for their children, that it's some kind of law of nature that all of their children should benefit from it equally and forever.

So many times I have seen where second generation businesses are run by one or two of many children, but where ownership of the business has been divided in many more parts, usually all equal. Often, the non-working shareholders may hold ownership and control equal to or greater than that held by the working successors who are inserting their own sweat equity to build the business.

A more fundamentally unreasonable situation is hard to imagine, and putting it all into a trust managed by Rasputins of various kinds, acting as trustees, doesn't solve anything either.

As you can imagine, I've seen a lot of strange

arrangements over the years. One in particular comes to mind. Grandfather "A" started the company. He had one son and one married daughter, and both the son-in-law and the son worked in the business. His daughter had one child, a girl, while the son had three children, one son and two older daughters.

Over the years, the son-in-law and the grandfather increasingly held hostile views, so the son-in-law quit. The son had stayed with his father (who died at 86), but never got around to managing much of anything because the grandfather, who thought his son was a weakling and incompetent, never really let go. When Grandpa did die, the son, then 58, took over and the oldest grandson, his grandfather's namesake, then just out of college, entered the company as a representative of the third generation.

In the old boy's will, he made his four grandchildren *equal* beneficiaries through a *per capita* distribution, i.e., a 25%, 25%, 25%, 25% split, upon the death of his wife, of all the company stock. Six years later the son died at 64.

Grandma, who worshipped the ground her only grandson and her husband's namesake walked on, directed that the young man be made president, and that both husbands of the two daughters (one of whom was an associate professor of biology at a local university, and the other was a self-styled wheeler-dealer who had already opened and closed four businesses) be placed on the board with him and her.

When grandma dies (she's 88 now) I don't want to be anywhere near that town. When two bitter sisters and an even more bitter cousin (as far as she's concerned, if her uncle hadn't poisoned her grandfather against her father, she would have received 50%--a daughter's equal share through her mother, instead of only 25% as one of the grandkids) combine their three quarters and get even with their greedy brother who's been doing the best he can without a lot of help, there's going to be one hell of an explosion.

INHERITANCE NOT A CAFETERIA

I've never seen any document that states there is such a thing as a "right" to a specific inheritance. A man bestows his wealth out of love and a desire to place a lasting gift of rememberance in the hands of his heirs.

It's true that the successful business founder has built wealth. But that's not what he leaves his children. Wealth by itself is essentially a catalyst, hopefully supportive of noble means. Often, however, it's destructive.

Of course there are economic reasons why we should want to pass pieces of our businesses on to our children. That's natural. After all, the best investment anyone could have in today's world is in earning power, and one of the best repositories for that earning power is a successful, growing business that we, ourselves, understand, own and control. But the business is only an *investment,* not a guarantee.

What we are offering to our working heirs is a financial advantage and some significant--but limited--forward momentum. These heirs are being handed anything but a worry-free existence. They are being asked to enlarge a dream, to wrestle with their own talents and limitations, and to struggle with problems much larger in scale than even we faced, as founders.

Every successor begins at his or her own beginning. They must make their own mistakes and create their own triumphs along the way. What they can be given by the founder is a foundation on which to build a dream and a powerful and effective tool--a *successful* family business--with which to build that dream.

This investment is not for everyone, even if that "everyone" is composed of our children. We do give gifts out of love, and we often give those gifts equally to our children because we love them equally. But a successful business is not a gift. It is a challenge. It is an opportunity. It is a commitment and dedication to the belief that something worthwhile can be built. A family business should not be treated as a gift, either by the donor or by the recipient(s).

We can leave our heirs their heritage in two forms: either as wealth or as challenge. The two are significantly different and must be given for different reasons. It is the responsibility of the founder, once he's accepted the need to divest himself of his worldly acquisitions, to do so with great care under the guidance of wisdom. To do otherwise would be a great disservice to everyone involved.

Wealth means opportunity. It is an advantage, the chance to start at a higher point to achieve even greater things than the person who built the wealth achieved. Wealth is an opportunity to do what the person wants to do, to have a chance to achieve what can be achieved. But opportunity is not an endless flow. It's a responsibility and it only comes at certain points in life. A legacy is one of these points.

For the heirs interested in and committed to the business, this wealth is the organization that gives them the power and ability to carry out their dreams, both personal and corporate. For others, for whom the business is not an interest, wealth is the opportunity to do other things. To give the challenge of the business to those who are not interested is irresponsible largess and an injustice to the interested heirs.

What future equity growth there is in the business will come as a direct result of what the active management does with that opportunity.

RECOGNIZE THE FAMILY TREE

There are infinite variations among families--e.g., daughters coming first, daughters coming later, many children, few children, sons-in-law, daughters-in-law, capable children, helpless children, interested children, non-interested children, second wives with children of their own, second families, ad infinitum.

Say there is a daughter who is the oldest and happens to marry a man who has good business judgment and acumen. Say, also, that there is a young son who is just entering college. There's no way that this father can assume logically that his son alone is going to inherit the leadership of the business. If there are more older daughters, the founder will have to deal with more known sons-in-law before his son is ever ready to prove his worth.

This is why it is so important for us to recognize, very early, the pattern that our family is taking. We must recognize the facts of the relative ages, maturity, experiences, talents, interests and abilities of our children, as well as of our instant family as they grow or join us.

It's crucial actually to put the family tree down on paper in some organized way, and keep it up to date because it's on this tree that the leaves of our legacy are going to be distributed. Since that distribution must be related to the needs of the company, this chart can help expose potential mistakes, or predict obvious reactions.

Statistically, the mates to our children will tend to be all established before we meet our maker. If only we could have had this growing up occur as much as possible under others' eyes, as well as ours, to help us make this (usually irreversible) decision with as much enlightenment as possible.

I realize there are airplane accidents and automobile accidents that claim fathers far too soon, that there are illnesses that create lingering needs. Again, as I have said, one must pray against catastrophy, but one certainly should *plan* against eventualities. This chart can help expose potential problems or highlight obvious selections.

In one company that comes to mind, there is an older son born to a relatively young father who is brilliant and able. This son is a hard worker and loves his father. He also has a much younger brother who enjoys working with him. A situation like this offers a real possibility of an acceptable business heirarchy, if only the future wives of these two single young men can be shown that their husbands admire each other, and that cooperation, not jealousy, has been their upbringing. Let's hope that Dad remembers to "share his dream" when these two young ladies join the family, for the needs of the young families must be accommodated within the heritage of their father's business with love and collaboration, rather than with mistrust and jealousy.

How different this situation is than that of another company where three daughters were born to a man late in life through a second marriage and none of them, at 15, 18, and 19, are interested in the business. He's now 61. He has to think ahead without emotion, and accept that his business is not likely to be run by his family in the short run in the event he is disabled. He must make plans to do what he must do while he has the time and the energy to do so.

Unfortunately, most of us keep waiting for the prodigal, whether the prodigal is a wayward son, a non-existent son-in-law, or the belief that somehow our talents are going to keep our youthful energies alive. We all must think ahead clearly. It takes help. It's a very hard thing to do. We somehow don't seem to pose the questions to people that can help us until it's too late. We somehow have to think ahead. Most surprises needn't be.

Fifteen years ago, for example, I got the bright idea to plant some willows on my property. I looked out into my back yard from my den and thought, "wouldn't two of them be just right, there and over there?"

I went out and bought two saplings about three feet tall and planted them in carefully chosen spots 20 feet apart. For the next 10 years they grew like only willows can grow. They looked beautiful. I watched, happy and contented from my favorite chair until what should have been obvious *became* obvious--the trees were starting to overlap and they were only half grown.

I got a book on trees and looked up how large willows can get. I saw that within 20 years they could expand to over 30 foot diameters. My amateur landscaping plan was destroyed because I didn't take the time to think about the future. All trees grow, some faster, some slower.

This sort of problem is very common in family business--only instead of willow trees, we grow family trees. Instead of branches we deal with stock. There are many stock distribution plans that look very clever today, and they are proposed by people who should know--the lawyers, accountants and trust officers who have spent their professional lives getting to know the vast intricacies of the tax laws. But too often instead of taking their advice as just that--technical advice--business founders tend to ignore their own judgment and follow the prescriptions of the professional "Rasputins" uncritically and with great eagerness.

TAXES AREN'T EVERYTHING

Of course, the tax savings are often very real and immediate. The consequences for the business may be good, too, in the early years, but given time, stock ownership can resemble the flu. If it isn't contained, everybody starts to catch it. It multiplies--or more accurately, divides--and becomes a major menace.

It may make good tax sense today to give some stock to the children. Or maybe the founder wanted to bring in some key men with expertise he needed but couldn't afford. So he gave them some stock. Then there was the employee stock ownership plan, or the stock he gave to the lawyer instead of cash, so he could get incorporated.

Later, as the founder becomes more successful and mellows, his attitude toward money mellows. Under the powerful influence of his love for his grandchildren, he begins to think it would be a magnificent philanthropic gesture on his part to give out little blocks of stock to them, and maybe to his long-term employees, in appreciation. Of course, because he has tax advice, he's encouraged in all this because everyone agrees that the best tax move is to gift it all to the kids early on, thus saving a bundle in taxes.

But those are *today's* considerations. What situations will these actions produce in the business after the founder has met his own bottom line? Just consider what can happen:

A *per capita* stock distribution to the grandchildren will result in each grandchild inheriting equally. The intent was to leave the business to our children, using the grandchildren's lower tax brackets as a vehicle. Trouble is our children aren't usually equally fertile and the family with the largest number of grandchildren winds up with more stock and more control. On the other hand, had the stock been left *per stirpes* --equal shares per family--that may have concentrated effective control of the company in the hands of whoever was lucky enough to be an only child. It's unlikely that either of these outcomes were the founder's intent.

Let's say further that the key man who got 20% died, as most of us are wont to do, and his wife inherited his block of stock which wasn't restricted because nobody told grandpa what he should do about anything, and then she remarried. Now she--and her new husband, a dentist--attend every board meeting conducted by the harassed successor-president.

The start-up lawyer may no longer have any relationship with the business for some very good reasons, but he will always manage to insist on wielding his 5-10% whenever the opportunity arises. With the remainder of the shares in a couple of big, equal blocks, his is the swing vote. This gives him a real power position from which to press his own advantage.

Or what about the involvement/influence of the 20% that was distributed all over the lot in decimal-sized blocks by Grandpa?

After it's had some time to grow, the shareholder tree is beginning to look more like a bramble--the family business has become a private corporation owned and harassed in varying degrees by a crowd of people the successor management hardly knows. That's getting pretty close to the definition of "public," without having any of the benefits.

EXTRAPOLATING ON TODAY FOR TOMORROW

What's needed early on is just a little bit of arithmetic. We can look at our family tree and see that in, say, 10 years there are going to be this number of kids at various ages. That's not a very complicated thing to do. Then we can guess what's going to happen by simply adding numbers and logical progressions over the coming 100 months.

A 20-year-old daughter in 100 months is going to be nearly 30. She probably will be married and is likely to have two or three children. That's not an unreasonable assumption, and it leads directly to some very important questions. For example, what will be the ability and interest of her spouse? How well will he get along with the other sons-in-law and the other children? Is there a chance that he may want to join the company? Will there be room for him?

Naturally these questions can't be answered before the young man actually shows up and we can see what we got, but the very act of *asking* the question can lead to a whole range of implications and suggestions for actions we can take now, while we're waiting.

In the case of the son-in-law, for example, it would seem logical to start in right away doing everything possible to assure that there will be acceptance and accommodation among everybody in the family when and if he does arrive.

We can't put off our estate planning until all the facts are in and all the loose ends are neatly stitched and tucked away. This is one of the truths many business owners are unwilling to face, like the people who refuse to write a will because they believe that means they are going to die. We may have a natural tendency to procrastinate, but it has to be overcome.

I prod myself to tidy up my own affairs by constantly imagining that next week somebody is going to say, "wasn't that great, how fortunate that he had a premonition." Well, it won't be a premonition. It's just a matter of keeping an orderly house because I *know* that someday I'm going to have to leave it in the hands of others, others whom I've taken the time to know and understand as best I can. Each of us, in his own opinion, dies "prematurely."

It should be on the basis of this kind of knowledge that the future shareholders are selected. When you leave shares, you are going to be leaving power--it comes with stock. When the founder leaves, he will be leaving power distributed in some way. *Some people will inevitably be more equal than others.* (Whoever it was that said, "Misers make lousy parents, but great ancestors," must have been an only child.)

There are volumes written by technical professionals who update their thoughts with each revision of the tax code. But, we must remember that the purpose of these guides on estate planning should be not just to disinherit one miserable relative (Uncle Sam), but constructively to bequest our earthly possession to do good for our loved ones. I can't think of a place or time when more good (or harm) can be done than in the attempt to dispose of the management and ownership of a family company.

This is where the only advice to take must come from the best advisors and directors we can find, who can combine both compassion and love with corporate responsibility and opportunity. I know advisors and directors like that are hard to find, but likewise, it pays to wait to find the right choices. We can't wait forever putting it off, saying a better one will come along. Sometimes it's put off until no one wants us or what we have isn't worth it.

One founder I know has three sons. Though the older boy is more sensitive, the younger two are more talented in a business sense. The older boy has a more agreeable wife than either of the younger two, but they all get along well as brothers-in-law and sisters-in-law, even when no one is watching.

These are all very different people, yet the founder is willing to leave the business in equal thirds to these three hard working, interested brothers and their wives. And, he has been implementing this plan in advance by careful management, development of all concerned and the creation of an accepted management heirarchy which responds to the needs of the business as he sees the needs in the future.

He has, by his own acceptance of their review, made his sons realize the benefit of the working board of outside directors that he has created to act in the role of being a surrogate father.

He understands the ramifications of equal share distribution. One very effective way to make sure that squabbles among disagreeing siblings have the power to destroy the business is to leave ownership in equal distribution, where no one of those siblings has been given control, and where no accommodation or conflict resolution device is available to those involved.

Equal distribution, be it between two brothers or among a number of children can be a license to fight if there is not a strong accommodation and acceptance among those heirs. On the other hand, unequal distribution, if unwisely handled, can create dissention from the start. It's a tough dilemma to have to face.

I know of another company, for example, where the oldest four boys were in the business and constituted the board of directors. While the founder was still alive, the most talented of the four was president. When the founder died, leaving the ownership to each of the four brothers equally, the younger three pooled their shareholdings and kicked the more competent brother out of the presidency and out of the company. I'm sure this outcome isn't what the founder intended when he designed his estate plan.

Whatever plan a founder chooses, one thing is sure. He will someday have to make one of his heirs president and the others something else. He can't duck the issue forever, as some business owners try to do, by making each of them a vice president. No matter what is done, one of the sons will have to have a little more right to the last word than the other, even if the ownership is distributed evenly.

The goal every founder must constantly keep in mind is

continuity , not tax savings. Continuity has its own demands, demands which must be given thought and acted upon if the business is to survive past the first generation. The decisions which have to be made are subjective concerns in many ways. They depend on the needs of the owner-manager and on the readiness and capability of the people involved. They are only secondarily *technical* questions. No amount of expertise in law, accounting, or financial planning, alone, is going to be sufficient to direct these decisions.

It takes a lot of wisdom, courage, preparation, love...and prayer.

III

THE PERPETUATION

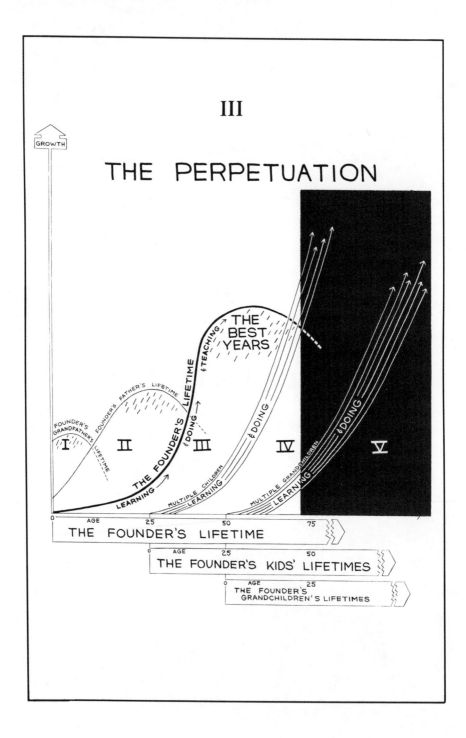

Chapter 9

Fairness, the IRS, and Family Feuds

*At this stage in the life of the business--more, perhaps,
than at any other stage--love, accommodation, and
understanding among the heirs become important to
keeping the family working together. Problems arise when
inheritors are of the opinion that it is their right to pick
and choose, by their lights, exactly what they should
inherit. What is "fair" is not always what is best for the
business.*

If we assume that our society will continue to oppose
confiscation of property, we can safely assume our success will
create an accumulation of material things. It's a fact of economic
life. Wealth, in some senses, however, is like waste.

Waste disposal is a problem in our society. We generate

tons of garbage, scrap and trash. Primitive societies don't have that problem because they don't really do anything that generates enough waste to worry about. But our society does. It is caused by our very success and that same success causes still another disposal problem--accumulated wealth.

The vast majority of the people in our society leave very little--maybe a house, some insurance, a couple of cars, furniture, and some family heirlooms. The value isn't great, in general, but there's a lot of strong emotion involved. People have the most horrible fights over who's going to get mother's napkin ring or the chipped mirror in the basement. The value in economic terms doesn't really matter. It's the intense emotion that fuels the violent struggles over inheritable property.

Now consider the small percentage of our society who have something very significant to leave behind. In these cases, high value is added to strong emotion and the fire is fanned into an inferno. If the struggle is fierce over Dad's old watch that hasn't worked for years, just consider the battles that can rage around "control" over major material wealth and the means to generate it: a family-owned business.

IT HAS TO GO SOMEWHERE

Wealth isn't destroyed when the wealthy die. It won't just go away, so it has to go somewhere, and there are only so many options. It can be distributed by default, of course, by simply doing nothing to settle the estate. In that case it's essentially given to the government, a persistent, greedy partner who will maximize his take in direct proportion to the lack of attention that is given to him.

Uncle Sam, under those circumstances, takes his considerable share, then allows those bits and pieces that remain to be distributed--in some pecking order of widows, children, second wives, cousins, and so forth.

More often, however, at least some planning is done,

however minimal it may be. The founder, forced to make decisions based on tax laws he doesn't understand, puts the whole future of the business in the hands of a series of professional Rasputins who may or may not give him good advice. This is called "estate planning" and it's one of the major growth industries of the decade.

Every day I see more printed material than I can read on tax shelters, gimmicks, tips, advice, strategy and the like. Most of this material is aimed at "tax avoidance," which is the name polite society has for "beating Uncle Sam."

I have no quarrel with trying to minimize tax liability in itself. That's an important factor in management planning. Its justification, in theory, is that it increases the amount of cash available to the business to meet its needs in the future. But almost inevitably this praiseworthy goal turns into a holy crusade to not let the government get *anything.*

(This is not the place to take to account defense spending, welfare spending, mismanagement on Capitol Hill, and greedy bureaucrats. But at some point a non-involved outsider might make somewhat similar accusations about the business owner's extravagance. The business owner, of course, excuses his actions on the basis that, by God, it's his (?) money and he can do with it what he wants.)

I'm not interested in discussing the morality or social utility of profit. My point of view is that profit is like health--and there's no way someone can have too *much* health. But, just as the purpose of health is to give strength to a life of accomplishment and contribution, so is it that the purpose of profits should be to assure the continuity of the enterprise and the good it can do.

The problem arises in the family-owned business when there develops a *preoccupation* with profits. This can happen all too quickly, because in these businesses, profits are usually equated with income and benefits to the owners. This preoccupation creates economic hypochondriacs.

Since taxes take such a huge bite out of "profits," they can quickly become an obsession, to such a point that the future good of the business fades from consciousness.

It's really simple to cut our tax bill. All we have to do is run the business into the ground, fire the employees and padlock the doors. Stop making money and we'll never pay another tax dollar as long as we live. Neither will our heirs. We will finally have the IRS off our back. *Liquidation is the ultimate tax shelter* .

OL' IRSU

There are other ways to look at taxes and the IRS besides with horror, although most of us don't seem to realize this. Everywhere I go, whenever business owners talk together about the great threats that are destroying American free enterprise, I hear the word "taxes" and the grumbled letters, IRS.

There's little doubt that the present tax laws are not the happiest we could have, and that some major redesigning is necessary for the long term good of the free enterprise system. There's also no question that Uncle Sam is one of the greediest and most long-lived relatives any of us are likely to see in our lifetimes. He seems to loot the business community with the impunity and glee usually attributed to Attila the Hun.

But, in fact, the tax laws and the IRS have probably *saved* more businesses than they have plundered since the 16th Amendment was added to the Constitution. For one thing, *the IRS provides business owners with a required course in accounting* .

Left to their own devices, most founders would probably have settled for the back of an envelope and some dull pencils, but the IRS has little patience with smudged notebooks and eraser crumbs. The IRS requires *accounting* , not simple record keeping; and the business owner, with a lot of weeping and gnashing of teeth, eventually is forced to comply with those "unreasonable" requirements.

The lesson doesn't often take, however, because the business owner resents it so much that he never graduates to an understanding of how much good an accounting system can actually do for him. All he sees is its potential to confuse the IRS. Although every business founder is forced to attend classes at ol' IRSU, like most unwilling students, he spends most of his time figuring out ways to con the teacher and pass the course with minimum effort. He, consequently, comes out with a minimal education though the tuition is high (it takes half of what you have). There are even some foolish people who don't benefit at all from the course. They just keep trying to fool the teacher and get by with minimum work.

This is a shame for a number of reasons. For one thing, accounting is the only language through which a business can be understood, discussed, and defined with any objectivity and accuracy. Tax accounting may only be one dialect in this language, but it's better to have a dialect than no language at all. In many businesses, we have the IRS to thank that the managers can speak "business" at all.

But the education from the IRS doesn't stop with accounting. The tax people also offer a course in contemporary social studies. It may not be as immediately effective as the accounting course, but it covers some very critical issues that are important to business transition.

Tax people and others without them take a dim view of corporate yachts and two-week "board" meetings on the Riviera. This may seem, on the surface, to be an unmitigated invasion of privacy and perogative, but it often has the beneficial effect of saving the golden goose--the business--from a prolonged abuse and potentially fatal bloodletting.

The IRS also has this strong prejudice against salaries for relatives who don't work--or paying them more than they're worth on the open market. The tax people can be fooled, of course, but on the whole their presence on the economic scene provides some necessary and healthy discipline for any business.

Taxes are a major factor in estate planning, but chiselling Uncle Sam should be anything but its major objective. Uncle's not really the business's worst enemy anyway. In fact, in his own peculiar way, he constantly encourages some pruning of the family tree by objectively defining what's "fair."

EQUAL ISN'T ALWAYS FAIR

There's a family-owned business in the Southeast in which the three working brothers are paid equally and have equal perquisites. Their individual contributions to the business are as unequal as they could be, but since each holds 25% of the stock, the reasoning is that each should get equal benefit from the business.

The other 25% of the ownership rests in the hands of a sister who works part time in the office. She's married to the head of the parts department and her salary, together with her husband's is carefully adjusted so that the sum of the two amounts equals what each of the brothers get. Those adjustments are usually upwards.

The objective may be to be fair, but it's no way to set compensation. You can bet that once this situation comes to the attention of the IRS, they are going to have some strong opinions about how "fair" it really is.

A profitable business ought to have enough for everybody, but most family-owned businesses too often just don't have the necessary advice available to work out a system of maximum rewards. So they get it done by the only systems they know--through salary and, ultimately, through equity distribution. "Fair" is made equal to "equal," and this is how the limited pie is usually sliced.

Since the aging founder wants his growth in bite-sized chunks (called "controlled" growth), he minimizes the expenditure of new energy and stunts any possibility of *real* growth. This is why the pie is limited. Small wonder why everyone falls on the carcass of the poor business in order to get theirs first.

If growth can be created so that the opportunities, and hence the rewards, increase, then obviously it's very shortsighted to take the view that everyone has to get his before it runs out. Business hedonism is a pretty expensive way to live.

I keep coming back to the tax laws, because in many senses they represent the collective wisdom about what is fair. The tax people have some very definite rules about payments for contribution. They differentiate inheritance from compensation and stick fairly rigidly to their guidelines.

The tax laws, and most of our society, see inheritance as a one-time gift bestowed upon an heir out of the generosity and love of the giver. Nothing in the Internal Revenue Code says that an inheritance has to be *earned* to be acceptable.

But compensation is something else entirely. It's shot through with the notion of "earned," at least in the minds of the tax people, and it comes under a whole different category of rules. This distinction, however, is often lost on the members of a family owning a business. Instead of looking upon the benefits that come from operating a successful business as *compensation* for effort expended, and the opportunity and advantage provided by the business as the *inheritance* , the two are confused in everybody's mind.

SOME SAD EXAMPLES

Ownership of an industrial distributorship on the West Coast was left equally by the founder to his three children. I met him briefly about a year before he died (he had an automobile accident), and he explained to me then that this was the only way he could be sure his children would know they were loved equally.

We discussed some of the problems I saw in the arrangement and he admitted at the time that maybe there was a better solution. But he never found the time to give the subject any more thought, much less to talk it over with his heirs or with advisors whose opinions and abilities might have helped solve his problems.

Now the company is owned in equal thirds by the younger son, who is also the president; a daughter, who is married to an architect and not involved in the operation of the company; and an older divorced son, who works in the business as one of the company's truck drivers. The president, a shrewd, aggressive CEO who is well respected in his industry, won the distributorship of a major national equipment line after a long struggle.

To handle the proposed expansion, the business was going to need all of the earnings it could keep, but the sister and older brother wouldn't go along with the plan. The source of the conflict was the sister, who--in league with her sophisticated husband--realized that any expansion would only dry up her accustomed dividends, while increasing her president-brother's income.

Because the older brother is single and financially untutored, she was able to convince him that the expansion would only be beneficial for his younger brother. Since his short-term objectives are to have more ready cash than his wages could reasonably provide, he joined forces with her to oppose the expansion.

Together, they were the team with all the power, and the president was left frustrated and powerless as a minority owner. Needless to say, these three siblings are no longer on the best of terms, (and, incidentally, the new supplier eventually cancelled his franchise since the company was only giving lip service, not support, to his product line.)

What is "fair" in this the Midwest, was left in thirds to a widow and two sons. At the time of the founder's death, the older brother had been president for six months, an arrangement that was acceptable to both brothers and the founder. The older brother had worked in the company for over 10 years while the younger brother was working in various marketing jobs at General Foods.

When the founder died, the younger man left General Foods and took over the sales department of the family baking company. It soon became apparent that the older brother was over his head in the president's job and the young man automatically took over more and more of the CEO's responsibility.

The founder's widow, however, had never forgotten that her younger son had refused to come to work for his father when he was first asked, preferring instead to work for "strangers." The older boy was "loyal" and he was "there when Dad needed him." Besides "he's been here longer and knows the company better."

In her mind the older boy is the natural choice for president. So he stays on in the job, at his higher salary, while the younger son carries the load with increasing bitterness. He can't sell his inheritance because the older brother says the company can't afford to reacquire his stock. He can't leave and work elsewhere because he is convinced his older brother would destroy the business within two years, and his share of the business would be valueless.

What is "fair" in this situation?

As a final example, consider the case of a car dealership in New Jersey which was left 100% to the successor. The two other children, two married daughters, were given title to the company's real estate holdings, which included the showroom, service garage, body shop and used car lots.

In this case, the founder did not try to be equal. He just did what he thought was fair by giving full control of the company to his only working heir, and a source of steady income to his non-working daughters.

Actually, at the time of the founder's death, the real estate far exceeded the book value of the dealership itself, including the inventory, and the working brother seriously considered contesting the will when the estate was going through probate. Instead, he plowed his heart and soul into the business and in five years expanded it to three other locations and opened a growing truck leasing division.

The sisters, who naturally were very happy with their inheritance in the beginning, now have watched the business that was left to their brother almost triple in size, while the property that was left to them steadily declines in value because of its central city location. Now they have grown bitter with the feeling that they were short changed by their father. They refuse to have anything to do with their brother, who they feel has taken advantage of their father and of them.

Was the founder "fair" in this situation?

I would defy anybody to come up with a definition of what is fair, but I do know that "fair" is not necessarily the same thing as "equal." The examples I've given, as well as hundreds of other examples I could have described, make it clear that fairness is not *guaranteed* by any form of distribution.

FAIR IS WHAT'S ACCEPTED

Fairness doesn't lie in equality. It doesn't lie in the intent of the giver. Over and over again I have seen that what is fair is only that which is *accepted* by all parties involved as fair. It helps, of course, to divide things in such a way that we are as even-handed as possible, but no matter how morally right and well thought out our plans are, if they are not accepted by the recipients as being fair, then they are not fair. And this is an attitude which must be instilled from the very beginning among the siblings, that what their father and mother do in the management of their affairs is fair by the simple fact that Dad and Mom did it.

When we leave wealth to our heirs, in whatever form we may leave it, we are giving them advantage and opportunity. Wealth has no real life of its own. It is only a tool, something to be used in order to reach some useful goal. An inheritance is not a compensation for being a member of the lucky sperm club. It is a gift.

Our first step in assuring the fairness of our legacy to our heirs is to make sure the gift is given in the right form to the right people. The key to this seems to lie in the word "opportunity."

Since all people are different, what is an opportunity for one may have no meaning, or, in fact, may be destructive to another.

For young men or women who have a love for business and an aptitude to succeed at it, the *ownership* of a successful business would be an opportunity. It would be a far greater opportunity than, say, real estate or securities, because the successful business has an advantage the heir could *use* to advantage.

On the other hand, ownership of a successful business would not present an opportunity for a son or daughter who is interested in pursuing an academic career. Here, the interest, aptitude, and commitment needed to run a business are directed in other areas. Giving business ownership to someone in this kind of situation would be like giving a football franchise to a basketball team, or a violin to a pianist. In each case, the gift has some significant value, but presents no real opportunity to the recipient.

Wealth can be disposed of in many forms, and what form is chosen is best related to the person to whom the wealth is to be given. For opportunity to exist it has to be seen and understood--and accepted. This is what will make it "fair."

Fathers and mothers should not be surprised that their families, in most cases, are essentially completed by their early forties. There are, of course, always exceptions--late marriages, health problems, etc.--but, one usually knows in one's early forties the number and sex of one's children. And, so it should not come as a surprise as they grow that some number of them would not be interested in the business and would prefer not to be involved.

There can be available a 10 or 20 year period in which to make alternative plans, to acquire other forms of value than just the business. (As one wise man said, "the best way to get money out of the business is don't put it in there in the first place.")

This is all complicated by the requirements of the tax laws, of course, but once the business is preserved as an operating unit with working capital, there are lots of opportunities to put fixed assets and other such equipment in the hands of alternative activities. This can generate funds that can be kept separate for non-interested families. Wealth in it's own right can be created apart from the business.

This is not usually possible at the last minute without dire tax and organizational risk, but the period of time from the birth of the last child until the beginnings of the problem in the founder's late fifties or early sixties should be enough time to do the right things for a man who's willing to face the future before he gets to it.

EARLY DISCUSSION IS NEEDED

A warehouse distributor in the tire industry I met a few years ago struggled for a long time trying to decide what to leave to his two chilren. His son was working with him in the business, his daughter was married and living in the sun belt. He and his wife both felt that the business was their most valuable asset and tried for a long time to come up with a "fair" way to make sure their daughter received her rightful benefit from the business.

When I met this couple, they had already designed their estate plan to leave full ownership of the business to their son. Their daughter was to inherit the business property--the building and land--and would get a steady income out of the company in the form of rent. The couple's other, non-business property--the house, a collection of antique cars, savings, and so forth--were to be divided between the two children in equal totals.

We met and discussed their business and plans for the future a number of times on seminars. Our conversations got them to thinking more and more about the plans they'd made. It occurred to them, for example, that they had never discussed their estate plan in detail with either of their children, and had simply assumed they were doing the best thing for each.

Their daughter was married to a biologist on the faculty

of a small southern University, and she was building a career of her own writing travel articles on the places she and her husband would visit as he conducted his research. I asked her parents whether being a business landlord was what their daughter would value most. I also asked them if dealing with an absentee landlord was the best arrangement for their son and the business.

They answered frankly that they didn't know, and told me that they had already decided to bring the children together to get their point of view. It wasn't an easy discussion to have because the subject was based on the presumption of the parents' death, but they all thought it was important enough to make it worth doing. They held that discussion about six months later, when the family was together for the holidays.

Today that couple's estate plan calls for their son to inherit the entire business, including the property. Their daughter will inherit all of their non-business assets, plus they created an instrument of debt by the son to his sister which will balance the monetary values at a specific point of time. The company went through a financial reorganization to accomplish this under the most advantageous tax considerations.

The reasoning behind this new plan grew out of two considerations. Their son felt he needed to control the property to maintain flexibility in his planning for the future of the business. Their daughter and her husband felt that the financial ability to take a long sabbatical to pursue their careers was more valuable than a steady income, and the parents' non-business assets were more liquid than the business property.

The wealth being distributed to those young people is designed to be in a form that will provide the maximum opportunity to each. The son will have full control over the tool he can use to build his future, the business. The daughter will have the financial advantage to be able to remove herself and her husband for a significant period of time from the need to make a living so that they can both work at the things they love and do best.

There's no objective measure available that I know of that

would prove that this new estate plan is more "fair" than the original. But there is one thing that I am sure of--that family accepts what's being done as the best possible arrangement and I can't imagine a setup more "fair" than that.

Of course, I realize how difficult it is for people to bring up the subject of estate planning and the assumptions of death that it creates, and it has its difficulties. If a man tries to initiate a conversation on estate planning with his wife, she's sure that he has suffered a heart attack and isn't telling her. Whereas if she initiates the subject of estate planning, the husband starts wondering if maybe she has found a friend and is trying to tell him something.

Most important to the business in transition is the need to be sure that whatever is done is understood and accepted by everybody involved. Tax minimization is important, of course, because it enlarges the pie to be divided. The desire on the part of the founder to be as evenhanded as possible is understandable and commendable. But these two desires cannot be allowed to overpower the need to understand the true value of an inheritance, or the absolute necessity to avoid the situation which encourages resentment, disappointment, envy, and family feuds over benefits that can only be destroyed by a prolonged fight.

Something must be done with our wealth. The choice can be made by us, or it will be made for us by others. Either way the choice will be made. As much as the survival of the business depends upon competent management, the input of outsiders, and an accepted management hierarchy, it also depends upon the *wisdom* with which we give it all away.

Chapter 10

Releasing the Prisoners

*The very opportunities and benefits offered by a
family-owned business can often operate more like bait in
a trap than as rewards. When these benefits are bestowed
in the wrong ways, or at the wrong time, on the wrong
people, a cell door slams and clicks shut. A lot of cells
fill in this way over the years, and if they're not emptied,
their inhabitants can tend to become very frustrated,
dissatisfied, and downright troublesome.*

Sam is 52. He's now the controller of a Midwest printing
firm he joined after he left the Navy at the end of the Korean
War. It's been essentially his only job, a position he qualified
himself for through two years of night school in accounting.

Sam has one son who is in his first year at a nearby

teacher's college and an older daughter just about to enter graduate school. His oldest child, a son, is a graduate engineer working for a local architectural firm. Sam is proud of the fact that he's a self-made man, but he wants to work so that his kids can have a better chance at an education than he had.

Sam doesn't seem to have the energy he used to have, at least not on the job. He has a lot of time and energy to give to his kids and to working around the house on weekends. He also gets in a lot of trout fishing whenever he can. But it's just that his job gets him down a lot more than it used to.

Because the company has just gone through a couple of years of unprecedented growth, his responsibilities and the complexity of his job have almost doubled. In fact, he came down with his first ulcer a couple of years ago and his digestion is almost always bad.

He has appreciated the pay increases that came along with the increasing pressures, particularly now with two kids in college, but he hasn't been sleeping well lately and he's increased his smoking up to three packs a day. Sam can't really put his finger on the reason, but lately he's been dreading coming into work.

It might have something to do with the founder's son, 26, who has been working with Sam lately as the founder goes more and more into his "semi-retirement." Sam thinks "the kid" is too impatient sometimes, and that he doesn't really understand or appreciate the history of the company and how some of the systems evolved.

Sam is beginning to think he's going to have some problems getting along with the son, who's even started talking about bringing in a new outside accounting firm to help "straighten out the books."

A PRISON WITH MANY CELLS

Sam doesn't think about his situation this way, but he's a prisoner. He's a prisoner of his limited experience. He's a prisoner of the formal training he never got on the job. He's a prisoner of his age and of the comfortable salary he's grown used to--and knows he could never get anywhere else.

He's also a prisoner of the years he's spent under the command of a powerful, autocratic, erascible, and erratic entrepreneur, and of the fact that he's adjusted his personality and his work style to the founder's needs and expectations.

Sam isn't the only person in this kind of situation. There are, in fact, probably more "prisoners" in family-owned businesses in this country than there are in jails. These corporate inmates aren't behind bars or walls. They are not confined physically. But they are just as surely held against their will, in a situation that's neither good for them nor for the company. They come in many shapes.

There are the Sams, **the long-term employees** who are undertalented, misused, and often very much overpaid. These prisoners have few marketable skills and a personal debt structure that forbids any consideration of their quitting, and makes the thought of firing them seem almost sadistic.

Dad looks at the old guard and wonders what happened. Did the "Sam's" just become that way? Did he, Dad, help create this? Could he have spent more time in the development of his managers?

He knew (or should have known) when his children were born that Sam would still be there when the children grew up. Why wasn't the respect for Sam's abilities and experience created in the son? Why hasn't Sam accepted the son? Why hasn't Sam made it a point to train himself and train the son and have him understand that they've got a long and useful career together.

Did Dad poison the son against Sam by the cheap shots so often made in the child's presence about Sam's particular habits? Is the career of any 20-30 year old veteran who has given a lifetime of service to business owners always to end up being unappreciated by the young and overpaid by the old? Isn't there a better way? If Sam wasn't competent, why wasn't that fact made known sooner?

Again, the founder has enough problems in the marketplace with the suppliers and the union and the government. He doesn't want to precipitate problems. But those problems are going to happen, even if he ignores them now when there's more energy and time to solve them. They'll just happen later. People keep closing their eyes and saying it'll go away.

It's not just children that can be accused of glue sniffing. There's more conscious fantasizing at the owner level than would first meet the eye. They close their eyes to what they don't want to see, and since nobody else is there to make these facts obvious, they stay and fester.

There are **under-qualified sons or daughters** who came to work for their fathers after having neglected their education. "Who wants to study English Literature when I'm going to take over the family beer distributorship? Who needs to have an outside job when I can be well paid to do things inside? Besides, think of all the experience I'll get. My Dad will show me the ropes."

There are the **feuding brothers** who never got along, who are now forced into feeding at the common trough because it was the easy thing to do. They have no outside experience. They enjoyed living under the family roof. They never got a chance to test their mettle.

Every generation needs its own war. Not the bloody kind, fought with guns, but the struggle against odds that's fought with the spirit. Previous generations had World War I, the Great Depression, World War II, and a few undeclared--if vicious--skirmishes. Those of us who survived these experiences came through them greatly changed--just listen to our war stories if you don't believe me. But now, if we're lucky, we won't have depressions to teach the young. We won't have wars to teach the young. Instead, our children must get the sense of responsibility and personal creativity in other ways. I see one undebatable truth, though: The last way to learn self-reliance is to have a permanently feathered niche in the family nest.

There are the **sons-in-law** who came to work for their wives' fathers because it seemed to be the only immediate way to make sure their wives continued to live in the style to which they'd become accustomed under Daddy. It wasn't stated this way, of course. Dad probably stated it as: "Why not? We could sure use you."

Often, these young men had entirely different plans for their careers, but they leave pre-med, or teaching, or a job at a major corporation to join a family-owned business and a world they probably didn't expect.

Often they decide to join their fathers-in-law (and are hired) for many of the right reasons. There's the challenge of working for a growing closely held company and the potential of being able to take over a top job someday. The founder sees a bright young man who's personable enough and potentially useful. But even with all that, Ol' Dad can't ignore the fact that hiring his son-in-law is an excellent way to make sure his baby is taken care of the way only her Daddy can do it.

The poor son-in-law starts out with two significant strikes against him. First of all, his salary is more dowry than it is compensation, a fact he won't be able to ignore for too long. Secondly, his main security comes with staying sleeping with his boss's little girl, a fact the *founder* won't be able to ignore for long.

When sons are around, sons-in-law tend to stay vice-presidents.

A whole category of prisoners are the **other relatives and those who have been given minority blocks of stock** on the pretense or silent understanding that those shares will someday be worth a great deal.

Minority participation in a family-owned business can be a legitimate participation and investment--for those who actually have an active involvement in the management and direction of the business. Their reward is in the form of salary and a participation in the equity growth is a potent symbol of their contribution.

But for non-involved minority owners there is no salary. Because of the tax laws and the fact that the growing business needs all of the pre-tax cash it can get its hands on, there are seldom, if ever, any dividends. Because there is no "market" for a minority share in such a business, the poor minority owner can't even sell his or her shares to convert them into some kind of useable wealth. The only potential market are the present majority owners who may or may not see a reason to buy, at a price that may or may not be "fair."

This situation is almost guaranteed to encourage the minority owners to see their own self-interest in harassing the management, criticizing decisions, lobbying for dividends, opposing corporate investments, and generally fomenting trouble.

This creates a completely different category of prisoners, the **managing owners** who have to face this cadre of restless malcontents. If the managing owners are lucky enough to hold the majority of the shares, all they have to face is their sense of responsibility to the other shareholders and a lot of harassment. If, as often happens, the family management doesn't hold a controlling interest in the company, the business begins to resemble a prison riot.

There are **wives** who are prisoners, suffering through solitude and/or neglect. They are prisoners in a cell of luxury, surrounded by the marital golden handcuffs of two-carat diamonds, winter tans, and social position. They are prisoners of success.

Maybe the founder didn't want to burden his wife with his business concerns so he inadvertently cut her out of participating in his dream and sharing a significant part of his life. When she becomes his **widow** , as she is statistically likely to do, she may find herself totally dependent on a business which is strange to her and on advisors selected by her husband whom she never really got to know.

When her future was in the hands of her husband, at least she knew and loved who it was controlling her destiny, but with him gone, she may not know who is pulling the strings of her future, or why what's being done is being done. She is the prisoner of an insensitive estate plan, drawn by experts and signed into fact by a man who loved her. She has no guarantees she can believe that her future will be the future she wants.

There are **daughters-in-law** who suffer through their own particular brand of neglect--sometimes resented, often ignored. They are prisoners to the incessant demands placed on their husbands by the business to which they are committed, a business these young women do not understand and are not being helped to understand.

The daughter-in-law can be a prisoner of a set of conflicting loyalties. She is loyal to her husband and what she sees as his requirements. She is loyal to their marriage and their children. He is loyal to her, too, but he also has his commitment to the family business, to his father, and to the rest of his family.

His wife will support and defend only what she can understand, and if she can't understand the reason for the excessive demands placed on her husband, she won't support him in filling those demands for very long. If she doesn't understand where the business is going and what it will mean to her husband and her family, she will not be able to share his dedication.

She remains his wife because she loves him, but she feels hemmed in on all sides by the demands of a business she resents. She is a prisoner.

In both cases, these women become unwilling participants in an all-consuming dream they don't (or aren't allowed to) share or understand. They're not prisoners by intent. Nobody wanted to put them into their position. They are prisoners of circumstances.

Finally, there are the **other heirs to the founder** who were forced to join the business under pressure, overt or otherwise, from their father and the family. It was "expected." Or they were "needed." Maybe the family business was the only option they knew because it was the only option they were allowed to see. These heirs can become prisoners, too, because the family-owned business is usually a terminal occupation.

It's terminal for two important reasons. First of all, the experience gained in a family-owned business is usually not transferrable. Working for Dad is not usually a stepping stone to something else. Instead, it's a specialization, a narrowing of general business interest to a concentration upon one very important, but very unique business problem. It is an experience in which to apply general knowledge and skills, not usually one which makes the heir more qualified for more common and standardized management occupations. This makes it less and less likely, as time goes on, that the heir will be able to find equivalent work outside the family company.

This increasing unemployability, coupled with the common practice of overpaying family members, helps to slam the gate shut on the working heir.

The second important reason why employment of family members in the family business tends to be terminal is loyalty. In most any job, the people around the employee depend on him to do the best he can, but in the family-owned business, these people are also his brothers, sisters, parents and cousins. Their relationship with him goes far beyond business concerns and office Christmas parties. To let *them* down (by quitting, for example) often means a disruption of one's entire life.

Many times, the heir's seemingly only viable option is to hang around, trapped in an unfortunate situation out of love or respect for the founder and/or other members of the family.

For a whole range of potent reasons, many family businesses harbor a number of unwitting and unwilling inmates. They are all prisoners. They are all in a position where they could be enjoying the opportunities and challenges, the freedom and control a family-owned business offers. But there is no enjoyment. They do what they do under duress. They are unwilling and they feel put upon and mistreated. They deserve something better.

Just as there's no place in a closely held company for incompetence, there's no room for the unwilling, the uncommitted, or the bitter. These attitudes are like a slow poison which builds up in the system until the dose becomes overwhelming. Every business owner presides over one of these potential "prisons," but often because of his isolated position as The Boss, he's not aware of it.

More accurately, it's the *founder* who both creates the prisoners and remains blissfully unaware that they exist. The successor, on the other hand, very soon becomes very aware that he is serving as a part-time warden over the people incarcerated during the founder's reign.

It falls on him as another one of his urgent jobs to find those prisoners and do everything he can to release them.

Finding them isn't too hard. They make themselves known one way or another. It's *releasing* them that's the problem. Often they're like horses in burning barns, unwilling to leave. Even more often, they just aren't ready to make it in the outside world.

RELEASING OUTDATED MANAGERS

The long-term, less than adequate managers (like Sam, for example) have devoted their entire working lives--or at least a great portion of them--to the company. For them it's an essentially terminal occupation that becomes more "terminal" as time goes by. Usually they have been brought to their precarious positions by a series of misdirected management and personnel decisions.

Competent or not, there's a tendency for employees in a family owned business to become helpless and immobile--often because they have been sidetracked by the founder or frustrated in their ambitions.

If the founder has had a long tenure of, say, 30 or 40 years, the people that he brought in at the bottom of his curve have all gotten older, but not necessarily smarter. And the job demands are greater, but the demands on them to produce more have not been made, and the boss finds he has to compensate for the inadequacies of the employees. Also, since they are still younger than the boss, the boss still thinks of them as the boys he brought along, not realizing that they are (to his successors, at least) over the hill and of minimal value. Their 30 years experience is often viewed as fifteen years experience two times, ten years experience three times, one years experience 30 times, etc.

Entrepreneurial bosses have a tendency to inhibit their people, often refusing to let them work on their own and condemning them to second-class managerial positions. These employees can either become too scared to get up and get another job, or they feel they've been in the same job so long that their experience is out of date and irrelevant.

Often, they're right.

The hard fact is that a middle management job in a family company can turn out to be a real dead end for an ambitious man or woman. An employee of a family-owned business, who's done little else, just doesn't have the world's greatest chance to become a responsible manager for another company. That shift is more likely to occur during their 20's or 30's. Much after that, they tend to become prisoners of their job. They're *stuck* .

The successor is therefore often stuck, too. If he looks over his payroll, he'll often find that the older employees tend to group at extremes of the pay scale. Either they are not very competent and the company keeps them at low pay, while they haunt the place like ghosts--or, because of years of loyalty and ill-considered automatic raises, they are so *highly* paid that nobody in his right mind would hire them at their present salary.

They didn't come to be where they are by themselves. They had help from the company to which they've devoted their careers.

PRUNING DEADWOOD

Of course, there's the simple solution of throwing the so-called "deadwood" out on the street with severance pay for conscience money. But most founders and most successors are moral people with a sense of honor and gratitude. It goes against their basic grain to reward loyalty with disloyalty.

Instead of seeking a practical solution, however, too often the answer that's accepted is to do nothing and wait for the old guard to decrease by attrition (a euphemism for waiting for them to die on their feet).

In justice, these people deserve some sensitive handling and consideration, but long experience has proven that neither the business nor the people get much benefit from maintenance of the status quo. Maintaining the inadequate employee, unchanged, in a position of responsibility, slowly destroys whatever confidence and ability the employee may have, while it gives the wrong example to other employees and tends to erode everyone's productivity.

Readjusting or removing the prisoner-manager is probably one of the most difficult jobs the owner-manager must face, whether he's the founder or the successor. But it can, and must, be done. It requires some frank, but sensitive discussion with the employee and then some active help, either finding an appropriate level within the company, or a job that fits the employee's abilities elsewhere. Often this is not as difficult a project as it may seem.

After all, managers in their 50's tend to have career objectives that are greatly different from young men in their 30's. In the case of Sam, he would probably be most interested first in his job security, even if it meant a decrease in pay, and second in his ability to support his children in college and the lifestyle he's come to depend upon. He would probably also be anxious to relieve some of the intense pressure he's suffering in his present job.

Of course, every case is different. People vary. Situations are unique. But solutions can be found if they are sought with the right attitude.

The same goes for the other prisoners. For example, the "dowered" children can be assured of an adequate living standard in many ways that are much better than the employment of their spouses. Employment in any business, particularly an family-owned business, should never be based on anything other than competence and a desire to work. A business is not a cornucopia for wealthy kids. It's a fragile golden goose that responds poorly to any prolonged drain on its resources.

Children can be given outright gifts or other property to manage--real estate, trusts, investments--for a salary. Either way, the distinction between the gift and compensation for performance should be carefully drawn. If this maxim were followed as a rule of thumb in any employment/compensation situation involving family members, many of the problems I see every day would be cleared up.

MINORITY OWNERS

Minority blocks of stock for those not involved in the management of the business tend more to be sources of frustration than of wealth. Depending upon who is involved and why they have the stock, these shares in many cases can be retired through negotiation--for cash, preferred stock, or for whatever is acceptable to all parties.

But this usually takes a great deal of diplomacy and tact on the part of the owner-manager--who, in these situations, is almost invariably a successor.

Having an equity position is so often a "status" consideration. Shareholding in growing enterprises is so firmly entrenched in our way of life that there seems to be something un-American about suggesting that minority ownership in a closely held business may not be all that it seems to be. But it is a fact that for the uninvolved minority owner there are many, many more effective and practical places to hold equity.

A major part of releasing these prisoners from a cell they may not want to leave depends on, first, gaining their trust and, second, convincing them of the fact that their ownership is doing--and will do--them little good because of the nature of the closely-held business.

THE INCARCERATED SPOUSE

The situation of the prisoner-wife is probably the most uncomfortable of the lot, because she is intimately involved with the source of many of the problems: her husband. But because of that involvement, her situation is often one of the easiest to solve.

Wives should be active partners, if not actually in the running of the business, at least in the philosophy, the thought, and the concerns. They can be saved from the widow's prison through careful, understanding estate planning. But in so many cases, business owners come to me almost adamant that their wives don't need to know anything that we're talking about.

Since they have to tell their wives something, they tell them not to worry, everything has been taken care of. These men seem to assume that estate planning is a male activity and their wives don't realize, until tragedy strikes, how essential it is for them to be involved, informed, and prepared.

THE "KEPT" TARANTULA

The same essential point applies to the daughter-in-law, only in her case, it's not preparation for tragedy but preparation for success that's important. If she is going to share her husband's life in a way that makes her feel contributory as a person instead of an ornament that's kept, she must feel that she is sharing.

She must really understand the business and her husband's activities. She must help him work through his problems and concerns if he is going to continue to share them with her.

If this doesn't happen, the business and the problems will eventually become too complex to explain to someone cold. Then it can be too late and without an idea of what is really happening, she can instead become a prisoner to the fantasies of her own *capable* imagination.

THE UNWILLING KIDS

Finally, there are the children who joined the business for all the wrong reasons. These prisoners are much easier to release *before* they join the business than after they're in it.

Heirs should be encouraged to join the business, but only if they are given a full knowledge of what it entails and, if possible, with some career experience elsewhere to give them the ability to objectively compare a career in the family business with other options.

Outside experience has the further benefits of increasing the heirs' credibility with the non-family employees, as well as giving them some qualifications for other jobs in the event employment in the family business doesn't measure up to their expectations.

Ownership of a successful, growing family business can be one of the most fulfilling and enjoyable ways of life possible. Working for a successful family company can have many significant advantages over the less personal, more bureaucratized public company.

But all of these benefits depend upon the willingness and commitment of the people involved, qualities very seldom found among a population of prisoners.

Chapter 11

Someone with a Problem: The Successors

The founder's departure--through disability, unplanned retirement, or, most commonly, death--leaves a vacuum in the company and family power structure. That vacuum can be filled before his departure or after he's gone--but it must be filled. The future of the business, now grown far beyond its beginning, depends on it.

Eventually, inevitably, the sands in the business founder's hourglass run out, because the Good Lord's prescriptions apply as well to owners as they do to mere mortals. There comes a time when he is no longer around to run the show. Time passes, the sand runs out, and he leaves to meet his Creator. Sooner or later, the business he built will find itself without him.

What's done then is done. No matter how much thought he has or has not given to it, no matter how well or disastrously it has worked out, whatever he leaves behind is his legacy. The world he leaves belongs to those who come after him, his successors. For better or worse, they have the baton and are now carrying on his dream.

All that has gone before, all of the events I have discussed earlier, all of the good and bad decisions, now come to roost on the shoulders of the successors and the founder's widow. They inherit the restrictions, frustrations, and deficiencies at the same time that they inherit the opportunities.

It's a package deal, a deal they have to live with. As much as they may want to at times, they can't bring back the departed founder and set him up in a chair in the boardroom and beat him up because of what he did or failed to do.

Now is the time that all the clever tax-saving schemes flower--with a blossom that's not always a joy to behold.

The first major *fait accompli* to be faced by the heirs will be the distribution of the post-probate ownership. Where have the shares gone? Who owns the business and who runs the show? The two are not always the same. Often, these setups are unfortunate and so ironclad that the heirs can't get out.

What, for example, if Mother--now a widow--has irrevocable authority and suddenly starts to act irresponsibly, or starts listening to bad advice from questionable authorities? Who's to judge? What about young widows? Second wives? What about remarriage? Has she the power to say yes or no to management requests? What can the heirs do? Shoot her? What about widows with real talent? Who decides? Why didn't Dad?

What if equal ownership is left to two working brothers and a non-working sister, and no president has been selected? One thing will happen if the heirs understand and respect each other. An entirely different result will come about if they have failed to get along since childhood. My heart aches for those widows left unprepared because of Dad's reluctance to face up to the inevitable.

THE MISSING BOSS

If a clear and accepted heirarchy has not been set up prior to old Dad's departure, one must be worked out by the family. Family businesses can't operate like communes any more than they can as dictatorships.

Committee management may work in voluntary clubs, where the members have few vital interests and not very much to lose, but in a family-owned business, where committees are made up of powerful, emotionally charged relatives and side-picking managers, any *pro tem* majority is going to find it damned difficult to make their majority actually rule. The power in these situations (common stock) may either (1) be distributed so widely that no one group has enough, or (2) the teams keep changing sides.

A dictatorship won't work either, because a person who happens to have the power might wind up spending more time waving it threateningly over people's heads than in using it for the company and its needs. Without accommodation--the agreement to agree--effective control is impossible.

Often, conflicts smoldered beneath the surface while Dad was around keeping things under control (and underground). But once that inevitable moment occurs when the patriarch and founder is no longer around, the struggle explodes into full-scale battle. Because the requirements and the agreements were not worked out while his authority was there to encourage it along, the alternatives to agreement happen--arguments, court battles, paralysis of the decision-making process, and eventual collapse of the enterprise.

A competent management hierarchy is necessary in any viable business, but the family-owned business faces the additional requirement that that hierarchy be an *accepted* one. Each family member must understand the needs of the business as well as the needs, desires, and rights of others in the family.

When the transition doesn't work out, the blame is usually placed on the inheritors, but it's usually more accurate to say that the seeds of dissent were sown and fostered by the founder, consciously or unconsciously, in an attempt to be "fair."

What he often does in his attempts to treat all his heirs as equally as he loves them is to create prisoners to his wishes, entrapment for those who want out, and harassment for those who want in. Once he's gone, the prison walls remain, but the cell doors are all swung open and chaos reigns.

In one example that comes to mind, a founder had left equal shares of his distributorship to his working son and two non-working daughters in his will. His son was clearly to be the next president, having worked for his father in increasingly responsible capacities for over 20 years, but this founder, at the time he set his estate plan, wanted to be "fair."

While he was healthy and working he gave little thought to what he had decided and, of course, never bothered to tell his heirs of his plans. Then cancer struck. As perspectives do in that kind of situation, his began to change. Lying in his hospital bed, he called his son to him and told him he wanted him to be the next president and they arranged for the successor to buy all the stock. Since the stock provision in the will now was no longer applicable, he told his son to take care of his sisters.

IGNORANCE IS EXPLOSIVE

When the founder died and his will was made known to the sisters, all hell broke loose. Convinced that their brother had forced their father to sell, they contested the stock transfer in court. Mom was in shock as the family's dirty laundry was washed in public.

Even though the suit failed, the family has been destroyed. The successor, even with his sense of bitterness, feels deeply his responsibility to fulfill his Dad's last request to take care of the two sisters. Although he has full control of the business, his heart is not in it the way it had always been. How the next few years go will determine the future of many people. But Mother's heart is irreparably broken. There are very few aspects of family relationships that the founder can safely ignore.

The successors, in turn, have to understand that the top job is not all beer and skittles. It's not the only prize worth having, while the others are all piled somewhere in the back of the bus. The younger (or older) brother, who may be filled with ambition but doesn't have the talent has to learn to accept the older (or younger) brother who does. That goes for their wives, too.

Again, to repeat a point, most reasonable people might be more willing to accept a position other than "first" or "equal" if they felt that the choices made were so done by an outside group of directors who were diligent and conscientious in the discharge of their fundamental duty, i.e. the selection and support of a chief executive officer to manage the company.

Obviously, in the absence of such support the inheritors try to run the company from their biased and obviously self-interested viewpoint, and usually do nothing more than emasculate the incumbent. The sad thing is most family members on family boards don't even realize what sins they are committing, for they have no valid frame of reference.

The new president, the successor, should understand the tremendous price he's going to have to pay for being the one to make all of the decisions. Somewhere along the line, his health is likely to suffer, or his family life will suffer. The leader has a price to pay, and that's something all the siblings must understand.

OUT OF THE SUCCESSOR'S HIDE

A classic example crossed my desk recently. A fine company, making special foundry castings, was founded 30 or so years ago, and is currently doing $1,300,000 per annum. The founder died six months ago at the age of 74 leaving a widow, 78, and two children, a son age 40 with a wife and no children, and a daughter age 48, married and divorced twice with no children.

The 100% ownership of the company was left in trust for the founder's two children--in a trust administered by the two children as co-trustees and the daughter as executrix. The mother is to receive income under the founder's deferred compensation plan and, upon her death, the shares would transfer to the children in equal parts.

The son is well educated with some outside experience in engineering and sales. He has worked as his father's right-hand man for many years. Because the father's health had forced him to become "semi-retired" 15 years ago (in fact if not in name), the son has done most of the work in recent years.

Many errors were made in the process of having that 25 year old son pick up the threads of a business that wasn't run right in the first place. There were the usual combination of little old ladies with mustaches making meaningless financial statements three months in arrears. There was a succession of outside accountants who couldn't care less, didn't charge much, and didn't do much. There were questionable attorneys of convenience, and a branch banker whose primary goal in life was to increase his quota in car loans.

Now, upon the father's death, the daughter, who had always been on the payroll in some fictitious category in order to give her money to augment her alimony, started making noises about wanting a larger piece of the action. The son had earlier made an overture to his mother to buy out the entire business, but the sister got herself a Rasputin of some dubious quality to act as her intermediate. What *he* really wanted to do was buy in with the sister and not let the "kid" get anything.

Because the son was essentially brought up to pinch advisory pennies, he decided to maneuver the sale by himself. Although a very intelligent, keen, sensitive young man, he didn't really have the street sense necessary to consumate such an arrangement. The deal fell through, as is usually true in such cases of self-taught brain surgery.

His offer was a decent offer for the business as it was, but the sister felt that there was more. And, her advisor was convinced that they could have the whole thing. Now, the son is finally realizing that his marriage and his life are going to be deteriorating continually as the result of the financial pressures put on him by his sister and his aging mother.

It's no solution, in this case, to wish to resurrect the father from the grave and have him understand that he had other options than harassing his son by forcing him to share the business with his sister, who could not possibly have any interest in its well being.

It's easy to understand the thoughts of a 74 year old man who wants his baby girl (she's 48, but she's still his baby girl) to have something to remember her Daddy by. It's easy to see why he gave her stock without thinking much of the consequences, but any good lawyer--any good estate planner--could have told him otherwise. Of course, people like this founder rarely listen. His business was different, you know.

Today, the only thing the son can do is to get tough and slug it out with his sister as he tries again to buy out her beneficial interest by (1) cutting off her funds, by (2) making her aware of the fact that he is going to run the business as he sees fit without any concern for her, and by (3) learning to listen to competent advice. If she wants to create problems, she's going to have to do it out of her own income, he's not going to supply company funds to provide legal attacks on the company.

He's going to have to learn to live with the will and the trust "as is." In the next ten months or so, things are going to get pretty tough on this guy and his wife. He will probably fail to convince his mother that he's not just greedy and trying to do in his sister out of her "fair share." His sister already thinks he's an absolute SOB. It all could have been prevented.

It's because of this tremendous pressure to buy out the lazy partners, buy out the less cooperative family members, that a "get tough" attitude sooner or later falls upon many inheritor Presidents. It's not that the guy all of a sudden becomes greedy and wants to keep all the goodies for himself. It's just that, in his definition, he and his family have paid enough of a price.

He sees no reason to take just an equal share along with all the hangers-on. After all, he reasons, what he inherited was an opportunity that was worth a given amount of money at some point. But it's usually the value at the time of the founder's death that's the basis for later divisions, not later growth continued ad infinitum.

Value freezing has been forseen in the law and there are many provisions in the tax law to do so for the non-working members by recapitalization, allowing the growth to go to a more limited number of working family members. This procedure has been well established in law and in practice. It's amazing, however, how few people know of it--probably the result of not dealing with competent advisors.

EMOTIONS CAN RUN HIGH

I've seen business after business face power struggles among the heirs after the founder leaves the scene. The only referee left is usually Momma, whose interest probably lies more in keeping peace in the family than in doing what's right for the business, which is the source of the funds being fought over.

In one company, the founder's wife was left in control with three ambitious sons of (in my opinion) unequal competance in the management. Her solution was simply to turn the presidency into a rotating chair. She gives each of her boys, in turn, a one year shot at the job of president. I can't think of anything more destructive.

Most widows of business owners aren't prepared, emotionally or intellectually, to settle the succession problems their husbands tend to leave in their wake. The same can usually be said about the spouses of the heirs, particularly the daughters-in-law.

The daughter-in-law sees Momma as a "dragon" guarding the treasure, while Momma sees this "tarantula" in the sack with her son. These bad feelings reinforce each other and, once Momma is widowed, the situation is intolerable for everybody.

There are few more negative influences on new successors and the business in transition, for example, than the existence of embittered spouses. Even if the brothers agree to agree, the sisters-in-law may not.

"A's" wife may not like "B's" wife. Maybe she never did and never will. Try to imagine in those circumstances to what extent she will be able to accept "B" being president of the family business. It's her husband's name on the door as much as it is his brother's, even though he's younger.

"A" may be happy as vice president with his more capable brother as president, but "A's" wife says over and over again, "no way." Her main occupation becomes that of a professional agitator.

And each family starts fighting for *their* kids' rights.

These are almost unwinnable situations and they happen every day. Some people, of course, don't want to be boss. For them, being a lieutenant is preferable to being the captain. And if that's the way the hierarchy happens to work out, it's definitely convenient. But it's unusual.

Most people tend to want more than they have, whatever it is that they do have, and if they are not taught very early on that there is a limit to what everybody can have, the management of the company will wind up as a platoon of neurotic colonels, none of whom trust the other.

As if the struggle for power isn't enough, the founder often uses the business as a cornucopia for distributing his largess to children and other family members who seldom earned what they got. The heirs never learned to connect the idea of a dollar's pay with the concept of a dollar's work.

Believe me, when everyone is used to equal compensation for unequal contribution sudden accession to the top management slots in the business does nothing to change this fundamental flaw in their education. Why can't I be paid what you're being paid? That's the way it always was.

I have seen all sorts of imaginative, creative ways in which family members get paid salaries, fringe benefits, and perquisites from the family business on a pre-tax basis. Most everybody understands that dividends are not the preferred way to get money out of a company, so fathers feel that the name of the game is to outwit Uncle Sam by giving money to the kids. They usually discover too late that outwitting Uncle Sam has cost them their business, because the successors are eventually saddled with this ever more inequitable burden, to say nothing about the actions taken by the Internal Revenue Service.

The successors may be unwilling to continue the dole, but all the recipients have gotten *very* used to receiving it. The best way to eliminate welfare is to not start paying it in the first place.

It's always seemed strange to me how the fiercely independent entrepreneur--who fights tooth and nail against "giveaway programs" to the "unworthy and non-productive parasites" of society--doesn't realize how "welfare payments" to his family are equally irrational. Maybe because it's a way of bypassing the IRS that makes it seem okay.

THE PRECARIOUS TRANSITION

These struggles for power and perquisites are more bombs exploding in the foundation of the business, bombs whose fuses were set long ago during the formative years. *And the transition is the time when the business is least able to withstand all those little explosions.*

The power vacuum left behind by the founder is not only felt within the family. It is felt throughout the management team and, outside of the company, by the customers, the suppliers, and the other people who have worked so closely with the founder for so many years.

The non-family managers, as well as the family employees and non-working owners, all have a very great vested interest in the continued success and profitability of the company. Unless they are convinced that the chief executive officer and other top family managers are competent, they will become obstructionists, laying obstacles in the path of any decisions the management makes, reluctantly carrying out the orders that are given, and putting heavy pressure on the CEO to perform to a whole set of subjective standards.

In the case of the non-family managers, a lack of confidence in the family at the top can lead to indolence, insubordination, ineffectiveness, inefficiency, and insolence--or, in the case of competent heirs, after a while they just depart for greener pastures, leaving the family business, which needs all the talent that there is.

There's no such thing as a surplus of talent, there's just a shortage of opportunities made available to use it. The very best people leave, employees and family both, leaving the company worse off then it ever was. The proportion of deadbeats gets higher and higher.

If a viable succession plan was not put together and put in operation during the founder's lifetime, there naturally was no way for the eventual successor to demonstrate to people within and without the company that he or she was able to fill the founder's shoes capably and successfully, let alone demonstrate that he or she is capable of carrying the company into complexities and expansions beyond even the founder's capability.

Suppliers and customers tend to see the owner-manager's business as the owner-manager himself. The same is true, in general, of the bank that supplies the short term cash needs and long term capital sources for the business.

Who is this young upstart who has stepped into the founder's shoes? Will the business succeed under him? The banker has probably made most of the loans to the founder personally. He would never entertain the notion of actually lending to the business. Now that the founder is gone, he wonders, who is going to make sure the loan is paid back?

Suppliers get nervous about who is going to take care of their market share in the area. Customers will wonder whether they'll still get the service they're used to. Both may start to look elsewhere, just in case "the kid" doesn't work out.

This is why unplanned succession can be almost as disastrous as no succession at all. The business has grown a great deal since the day Dad founded it in his garage. In those days, it was his competence and the working of blind fortune that determined success or failure. But by the time he gives up the helm, the business is beginning to outstrip even his considerable competence. The problems of increasing size emerge and complexities arise for which there's no precedent in the history of the company.

The question for the inheritors becomes so much more than simply one of *their* competence to do the job. It is no longer an entrepreneurial business. It is a successful family-owned business and it demands strong and objective input from a variety of management sources, as well as from the successor.

This objective, outside management just doesn't suddenly happen. It comes about as part of a long-range plan. But long range plans are seldom made and too often the successors inherit an entrepreneurial business with a gaping hole where the entrepreneur should be.

Even assuming that the management hierarchy is settled and accepted in advance, assuming that the offspring of the founder--and his partners, if he had any--understand and are willing to work for the needs of the business, the transition is in trouble unless the new management is ready and has the necessary help to handle the problems of scale that arise with succession.

THE KEYS TO SUCCESSION

A smooth succession requires:

1) **motivated successors** who possess knowledge and experience beyond that of the founder;

2) **an organized team of key managers** who approach their responsibilities professionally and agree to accept the new leadership enthusiastically;

3) a group of **competent advisors,** who understand the business, know and respect the successors, and who are willing and capable of helping pilot the business through the uncharted waters ahead;

4) an **uncomplicated and rational ownership structure,** one which doesn't confuse inheritance with management;

5) **accommodating heirs** who can cooperate and work together or agree to separate themselves from the enterprise. Business is tough enough without having to pull your punches in order not to upset sectors of the ownership; and

6) the presence and influence of **a working board of outside directors** --a greater requirement, even, than there was for the founder;

These are the keys to a smooth succession. When they happen to exist in a business at the founder's departure, the successors only have to face the huge complexities and problems of ensuring that a successful, growing company continues to succeed and grow in an increasingly complex world. *If these keys aren't present--and, sadly, they too often aren't--the successors also face the monumental task of putting them in place.*

LEADERSHIP MUST BE ASSUMED

But we have to assume, at this point in the life cycle of the business, that all of the successor managers come to the business with their unique backpacks full of knowledge, experience, and talent. Not much can be done to change that once the business is placed in their hands. If they are competent and committed, the first hurdle is crossed. If they are not, I wouldn't hold out a lot of chance for the business to succeed for very long.

A business which has been successfully managed for one generation doesn't just disappear overnight. The momentum of the market place usually keeps it going. All the good people don't leave together. All the suppliers don't change outlets at once. All the customers don't change sources immediately. But it's a gradual erosion, gradual and irreversible at an accelerating rate until, finally in desperation, when the business starts throwing off large amounts of red ink, panic sets in, and someone blows the whistle.

Accommodation and agreement, if they don't exist among the heirs when the founder goes to his eventual reward, can still be brought about. But this requires leadership either from one or a few of the heirs, or from an accepted outside mediator.

I've seen it happen many times where squabbling heirs have been made to understand that their true interest lies in preserving the golden goose left behind by their father. They can sometimes see, once it's pointed out to them, that family fights don't increase profits and that unbridled greed, like bloodletting, eventually kills the patient.

Once people can be shown where their true self interest lies, they can usually learn to act in their own--and therefore the business's--best interest.

The difficulty lies in getting them to listen to the truth. Again and again I come back to the absolute necessity at this point in time for the firm guiding hand of outside directors. Few professional advisors can have the desire or the objectivity to wade into a family feud and bring about peace without injuring some of the protagonists or finding themselves in a conflict of interest.

And it's understandable why this is so. Long term advisors tend to see their contribution as simply remaining on as advisors.

It takes a very brave professional to say to his client, "I'm willing to risk our long term relationship, but I'm going to tell you what you need to hear. If hearing it makes you unhappy, well so be it. But my conscience is clear."

Experienced advisors have seen these problems over and over again. The big issue is the courage of their convictions and their concern about losing their customer/client. Too often, they feel the principle isn't important enough to justify that risk and instead, they just do what they're asked to do and become increasingly docile and, hence, less productive.

DIRECTORS AS SURROGATE FATHERS

Clearly, the protagonists themselves would have little inclination to listen to each other. With the authority of the father gone, about the only influence that will have a beneficial effect on the vacuum left behind is that of a more or less formal body acting, essentially, *in loco parentis* , in the founder's place.

But in most cases, the board in a family company--both while the founder is around and after he is gone--remains a pasture for incompetence, a Siberia for the managerially senile, a cover for greed, or a lever for self-interest. It's too often a place where advisors can get together, periodically and with legal sanction, to justify their own existence. It's too often a device whose only purpose is to generate fictitious events in order to minimize tax. None of the actions of this kind of "board" has any real value in ensuring the continuity of the business it has the fiduciary obligation to protect.

The poor successor is faced with the immense problem of filling his many roles--as shareholder, chief executive officer, and chief employee. There's no way this poor devil can have a sense of strategy because he's buried in the day-to-day struggle just to survive his untenable situation.

Shareholders may have ownership, but a stock certificate brings with it no automatic sense of strategy. Even if all the shareholders were to get together in a paneled boardroom, complete with charts and reports and projections, they still wouldn't necessarily have any sense of strategy. A management problem is vastly different from a shareholder problem.

If an outside board doesn't exist at the time of the founder's demise, many obstacles have to be faced before it can successfully be installed. It can be done, however. I've seen it done. But it's an absolutely backwards way to go about things, not to mention a hell of a situation in which to bring in outside directors.

The founder didn't want somebody looking over his shoulder, probably because he was afraid they'd usurp his power as the benevolent despot. So the outside board was not installed during his reign. The founder meets his Creator and the successor meets an absolute mess. There is no continuum of authority, no steady hand on the helm during the transition. The resulting uphill struggle can be almost overwhelming. But to the successor, it's a struggle that must be undertaken.

Am outside board isn't a panacea. There's little sense in creating an outside board when all of the other things need doing. There's little sense in putting in a board when the managers are incompetent, the advisors are inadequate, there's no internal control system and the family is hopelessly at odds. In those circumstances, a board can't really be expected to solve anything.

A formal board of outside directors is the strong wrapping around a carefully packed package. If installed early enough, around the right package, it can effectively function as the surrogate father, filling the vacuum left by the founder upon his demise. Believe me, it can be a big hole.

A TOUGH JOB...BUT IT'S HIS (OR HERS)

The successor to a company unprepared for transition has to juggle many problems at once. Often he inherits a feuding family, managerial deadwood left over from the founder's regime, professional cronies who call themselves advisors, and a firmly entrenched board of relatives, and hangers-on. The whole situation is like a semi-collapsed building where to move just one stick is to bring the whole thing crashing down.

Even the strongest, most competent successor in the world couldn't wade into this mess swinging like Genghis Kahn and expect to survive the result unscathed. Two things are required, even though they seem contradictory: *patience* and *action*.

Often, for example, there are individuals on the board who, for one good reason or another, are absolutely unremovable-- widowed Grandma, for example, who has *always* been a director, owns a significant percentage of the stock, and would be crushed if she were to be removed.

But I've seen too many successors--kind, decent, compassionate people--put off far too long the removal of directors because they just couldn't place themselves in the position of hurting these people after their long association. Some of them have known the successor since he was a growing boy and they just love to get together and talk about old times.

How do you, as a decent guy, get rid of these people when humanity sometimes takes precedence over the business? This is understandable. I would hate to meet a man who had the compassion of a piranha and could only think in his own limited self needs and the hell with everybody else. (Here again is a good reason for putting limited tenure on directors as opposed to a lifetime occupancy of a chair as inherited right. The basis for board selection should be contribution, but in any event it is best arranged with an agreement as to the limit of tenure. Then nobody gets upset when they're asked to leave. They weren't expected to stay forever.)

But, again, the successor must accept, along with the privilege and opportunities of his elevation to the presidency, the problem of dealing with some of the less pleasant aspects of the job. Along with privilege comes responsibility, the chaff comes with the wheat.

In situations like this, I've found that forming an "informal" board of outsiders (a "proto-board") may be an effective interim solution. Any successor struggling against the overwhelming odds of an unprepared succession must have the help of a firm, objective, and understanding guiding hand as he attempts to clean up the ownership structure, recondition the management team, evaluate the advisors, and, if he can find the time, run the day to day operations of the business.

ACTION IS REQUIRED

The successor must take *action*. The only time a problem is certainly unsolveable is when a solution isn't attempted. *Patience* is required because the solutions to situations that took many years to form don't come overnight. For humanitarian, legal, and sound business reasons, many needed changes cannot be put into effect right away.

Long-term managers, who've given their lives to the company, cannot simply be thrown into the street. They may have to be moved within the organization, but even that takes time. Cleaning up the ownership structure will take the agreement and cooperation of the other owners. Their trust and acceptance, especially in an unstable family situation, won't readily be obtained.

Advisors may be easier to change, but the determination whether they *should* be and the decision about who should replace them is complex and shouldn't be done in haste.

Finally, some inappropriate members of the board may just have to be waited out. Even Grandma isn't immortal.

All of these complexities and problems, of course, could have been avoided had the founder thought ahead and planned for his success and for his own mortality. But successors face reality, not could-have-beens.

If Dad, for whatever reason, didn't fix it, then the job falls upon his successor for whom a strong faith in the future is an absolute must.

THIS COMPANY SHALL CONTINUE FOREVER

Chapter 12

This Company Must Continue Forever

*The road traversed by the family business from the
beginning through the transition and into perpetuation is
a gauntlet of threats and dangers and potential missteps.
It's a road that can only be successfully traveled by
committed, informed people who share the virtues of
competence, wisdom, accommodation, and love. The
future can and must be planned for. Mistakes can be
recognized and must be corrected. Only the discipline that
comes from an understanding of the limitations imposed
by the precious gift of time will enable these things to
happen.*

I have a little sign in our office. It hangs on a cork bulletin
board for everyone to see. On an old blank stock certificate, in

big letters, are the simple words: *This Company Shall Continue Forever.* That little sign, I'm sure, is hanging on the bulletin boards of thousands of other privately held businesses, businesses I've had the good fortune and opportunity to become involved with over the past two decades.

I have had these signs printed up and made available to anyone who wanted them because I have a strong and lasting belief that those words represent the reason behind everything I do, and everything the successful owner-manager does. The attitude it represents is what drives the waking efforts of the business founder. It is the inspiration and source of dedication of generations of successors to that founder. It is the source of confidence and energy among the managers and employees. It is also the strength of our free enterprise economy.

My belief that the successful family-owned business can, in fact, continue, generation after generation, is the only reason for any of my writing, teaching, or consulting. But continuity is as difficult to achieve as it is rare, mainly because so little thought is given to it during the most important years, the early years of the first and second generations of family members. Who was it who said, "It is always hardest for those to whom it means the most?"

The family-owned business is not a thing so much as it is a *process* . People come into it. People leave it. It begins, grows, succeeds, merges, and evolves. It changes and the people in it change, too. But the past is prologue to the present--and a foreshadowing of the future.

It's like evolution. Few people today take the Bible literally and believe that man just appeared in all of his glory in an instant of creation. He was created through a process of trial and error, from very simple forms. Man was created, but not by a God in a hurry, or without a plan.

A DREAM IN PROCESS

A family business is a complex organism, too, one which also grew out of simpler forms. It has a life of its own, and, with luck, it will live beyond the powers and lifespan of the founder thru the talents and effort of succeeding generations.

The business owner, like all other things that God makes, starts with nothing. He grows, and then he ends with nothing. It's hard to believe at the height of his "talents" that when he meets his Creator--he leaves all he has acquired on earth behind. All of this happens in something we call a "lifetime." But while he is going through *his* lifetime, there are many others who are going through *theirs* : his parents and their parents, his wife and her family, his children, his grandchildren and their spouses, his key employees and their families--not to mention his own brothers and sisters and their mates, his partners and their family, his directors, his advisors, his customers, his suppliers, and his competitors.

All of these people will have some varying input into the business and their influence will make the business what it will become.

In its best sense, *the family business is a dream in process* . If it didn't represent the owner-manager's hopes for the future, if he didn't want it to live beyond him, many of the problems that I see every day would be solved in a flash. It's true with most any dream you can have--stop having it, and most of the problems connected with it will disappear.

People who aren't involved in a family business--and therefore don't really understand what it is and what it can mean--often wonder what possible difference it can make if a business does die with its owner. Why shouldn't it? He started from scratch, learned the hard way, and struggled to the top on the basis of luck, talent, and hard work. Why not let his kids learn the same lesson? It would probably be good for them.

As far as I'm concerned, this kind of attitude is glib,

shallow, and envious. These same people would be the last ones to say the *only* way to enjoy eating is to starve first, or that the *best* way to learn to appreciate a nice home is to spend a few years sleeping in bus depots. This sort of lesson isn't really all that constructive, especially when it's repeated over and over.

WHY WE BUILD

Let's be honest with ourselves:

The truth is that most of us don't work hard and build wealth solely because we love hard work or wealth for itself. Some do, but most of us build for our children and for our grandchildren. We try to build a world in which they will have more advantages and a better start than we did, because--despite all of our talk about "the good old days"--we know that the way it was when we started wasn't all *that* good.

There are, of course, a lot of economic reasons why we would want to pass our businesses on to our children. The best investment anyone can make in today's world is in the earning power available to us. And the best repository for that earning power is a successful, growing business that we, ourselves, own, understand, and control.

But beyond economics, the family business is the best means available today for building a valuable heritage for our children, a heritage which comes in the form of a responsibility instead of a gift. It offers the chance to begin at a point which progresses in opportunity and purpose with every generation, to build on the dreams, struggles and successes of our forebearers.

This is the dream that's being built and made real through the business the owner-founder began and built. This is the WHY of continuity. This is why we must understand all the multiple generations who share their lives with others in this entity called "the family-owned business." The dream is being built for--and is profoundly affected by--them.

The perpetuation of the successful family-owned business is important to *everyone* in our economy, not just to families owning businesses. Not only can these businesses continue forever, but we should do everything we can to make sure that they *do* continue forever.

THE SHADOW ECONOMY

It's a generally unrecognized economic fact that, although the publicly owned corporation is the *producer* of most of the goods and services in this country, the privately held company is the *distributor/consumer* of most of those goods and services. The owner-managed business accounts for over 99 percent of the almost 14 million business enterprises in the country. They employ over 50 percent of the nonagricultural workers in the private sector and account for more than 40 percent of the Gross National Product. That's almost half of the business output of the entire economy.

Think about what these figures mean. The IRS counted 13.9 million business enterprises in 1974, 3.4 million of which were beyond the proprietorship stage. More than 2.3 million of these were corporations. Of this total activity, so-called "big business", the few tens of thousands of corporations listed on the various stock exchanges or traded "over the counter", represent a relatively microscopic 4/100ths of one percent of all business, and only 3/10th of one percent of all corporations.

Our so-called "small" businesses form a true shadow economy--but it's one *huge* shadow. A drive through the commercial or industrial areas of any American city will quickly demonstrate just how visible it is. The family-owned business is only unrecognized because it is widely ignored, looked down upon, and--by some--despised.

FAMILY BUSINESSES ARE ISOLATED

In spite of their great numbers, business founders are isolated, insular and parochial. They don't share a commonality of business interest. Because their businesses absorb almost all of their energy, they don't take time to talk honestly and share experiences with each other. Because they built their success on luck, guts, and raw talent rather than credentials, they don't seek or receive recognition from the establishment press. They suffer from a managerial inferiority complex that's neatly reinforced by that insensitive classification, "small" business. Because of this sense of inferiority, they have little idea of the envy their independence and success tends to create in others.

These entrepreneurs struggle alone, mostly. And, mostly, they just don't make it. Twenty percent of them throw in the towel in the first couple of years. Fifty percent are gone by the tenth. According to U.S. Treasury figures, only 25 percent of the businesses formed between 1956 and 1973 survive today.

The family-owned business resembles the mule--hard working, productive, but sterile. They don't seem to be able to last past the first generation, their founder's generation, and their disappearance has major implications.

MUTUAL DEPENDANCY

Most of our largest corporations, for example, depend for their existence on a complex and interwoven network of independent suppliers and distributor/dealer/contractors. This is why these so-called "small" businesses have a collectively massive impact on sales and purchasing charts in the offices of the Fortune 500. Because of the drive and talent of local entrepreneurs, because of their roots in the communities they serve, because they are building their own equity, family-owned businesses are a major source of large market shares and robust revenues for the major public corporations.

Yet these major corporations find themselves watching, sometimes helplessly, but too often uncaringly, as their distributors and suppliers wink out all over the country. They disappear either through liquidation, which leaves yawning gaps in marketing or supply networks, or through buyouts and mergers, which remove control from the manufacturer and leave the future in the hands of others.

This is why it's so important to everyone that the successful family-owned business survives the transition to subsequent generations. Most manufacturers can exist in their markets only through their distributors and independent contractors. This means the private business owner is the last interface between the consumer and the public corporation in nearly every sector of human needs--and at multiple levels. A loss of distribution in an area is usually disastrous to any corporation, and most often fatal to the manager responsible.

This is why helping these businesses plan for their future more professionally should be of vital concern to any manufacturer who is dependent on privately owned distributors, suppliers, or service agencies. The demise of any distributor can seriously jeopardize the very future of that manufacturer. It is no longer sufficient for any manufacturer to limit his help to product and application information. To survive and grow, successful manufacturers must do everything possible to help upgrade the management skills of their distributors.

This isn't the easiest job in the world. Manufacturers and distributors generaly have different goals and very different views on growth. The sales manager, his superiors and his sales force are largely made up of organization men who have to climb to achieve. Their function within the company is to get more products out the door this year than they did last year. Their goal is always to grow, to produce, and to sell--always more and more.

But the owner-manager, once his business is past the *survival* stage, isn't under this perpetual pressure to go...go...go. His *capacity* to handle growth is limited by his own experience and the ever-present need for capital resources. These factors confuse professional managers. They are best at understanding each other. They were taught together and they worry about the same things. It's easier for them to do business with those who inhabit worlds similar to their own. They just don't understand this other world, the world of the business owner. They never did.

MUTUAL DISTRUST

For this reason, they usually don't have much empathy with, or understanding of, the problems of continuity in the family-owned business. They tend to look at that business as one owned by an aging male and/or his no-good kids, who just want to level off and enjoy the rewards of their achievements, who want to keep even without sweating an increase in sales or suffering a decrease.

This lack of understanding works both ways. Owner-managers tend to feel that neither the big corporation nor the professional establishment is to be trusted. Business owners, for that reason, try to maintain an arm's length relationship with people who are essentially their partners. They feel threatened by the slightest rumblings coming in their direction from public corporations.

This distrust on the part of the owner-manager isn't simply paranoia. The family-owned business offers us an instant course in ethnic studies. Most of these businesses were founded by the immigrant, the unemployed, the dispossessed, the uneducated. *It's within such "ethnic" groups that the majority of family-owned business in existence today had their origins.*

These founders, unassimilated by the Ivy League ranks of the organization man, had no other means of fulfilling their ambition for power and privilege than through the sweat off their own hands and the strength of the business they built by themselves.

Because of this difference, and the generally

custom-tailored business practices he develops out of sheer necessity, the business owner seemed always to end up as the little guy, the underdog, the one who never made it in the big leagues of organized management. He was the outsider, always sniffing around the bush.

He always felt himself a second-class manager and the more that he was told that he was second-class, the more he believed it. It was a self-fulfilling prophecy. When he finally made it, he tended to bluster in his own little world because there were others in it who were even more outside than he was.

Because of the founder's influence and power over his own world, because he is usually the sole teacher of the next generation, these attitudes and actions are often passed on to the successors like an inherited disability. And the successors can afford it less than the founder.

INTEGRATION WITH THE OUTSIDE WORLD

I've written at great length about the needs and responsibilities of family members to be open to each other, to understand each other, and to adjust to each other's needs. I've discussed the changing organizational needs of the growing business, the need to develop the management team, and to rationalize the organization chart. I've covered the founder's need to share his dreams and concerns with his family.

I've also discussed the continually increasing need for the input of competent, concerned professional advisors and outside directors. Every successful family-owned business has a growing need for help, advice, counsel, education and direction from outsiders. Without this help, even if the family is able to work together and commit itself to growth and continuity, the company most likely will not be able to survive long term.

The survival of any business, at whatever stage it may be in its life-cycle, depends on the success it has understanding and working with the outside world. Sales, profits, and growth all come from the outside. Mistakes, losses, and failure come from *inside* .

But too often the suppliers and outlets to family-owned businesses are insensitive to this need. Because their own organizational world is professional and institutionalized, they either assume the world is the same for their distributors/vendors/contractors/clients, or they ignore the question altogether.

Advisors to these companies too often don't understand either. *Accountants* , in general, are uncomfortable talking to the business owner, because they're not sure it won't rob them of that great quality called "independence." Independence to a CPA is like virginity to a bride. It's his source of credibility. It's what he certifies. Accountants tend to be afraid if they become too involved, too committed, to understanding, too involved in the moral judgments and trade-offs the business owner has to make, they're afraid they'll compromise their "independence."

Too many *attorneys* tend to belong to a closed society with its own secret rituals. They tend a little toward the mystical and often do an excellent job of maintaining this mystique. Lawyers sometimes tend to extend their advice far beyond the province of the law. Like all of us, they have opinions on a lot of things and, often, they're very forceful about them.

But the business owner is not too often buried in legal problems. He is usually up to his armpits in *human* problems, his and other people's. He has management problems to settle, priorities to establish, and family differences to reconcile--to name just a few. Often, the advice he gets from his attorney is *competent* enough, but sadly lacking in *compassion* or appreciation of the contingent costs (risks) he is asking his client to assume. They place themselves in the position where their advice sounds like it should be accepted uncritically, but too often they don't take the time and expend the effort to understand their client's non-legal, but very real, problems and concerns.

The *banker* , because he gets paid only when the owner-manager takes his money or gives the banker his money to play with, doesn't usually consider advice to be his product. He's often forced into the position where he doesn't want to hurt the business owner's feelings. He tends to hesitate saying anything that is going to upset his relationship with his customer.

He and his customer also tend to have different perspectives on money. The business owner knows how to *make* money. He's learned how to mix labor and material and guts and brawn and luck and bargaining so that he can end up with a surplus of receipts over expenditures over a given period of time. Too many bankers don't understand how to go about *making* money. They know well how to handle it as a commodity, but have little idea how to create it. Too often they don't really understand their customer's world.

The *insurance agent* too often sees the business owner as a mother lode to be mined for ever-increasing sales. Although the underwriter is perhaps in the best position of any of the advisors to *understand* the business owner's problems, and to encourage him to take the steps necessary for continuity, too often his vision is blurred by the prospect of immediate sales.

This lack of understanding by others, combined with the strong parochial tendencies within most family-owned businesses, tends to leave the founder, first, then his successor, facing their considerable problems alone. They either get no direction, inadequate direction, or misdirection from outsiders, and the whole situation is an incredible waste. The business owner needs help badly. His suppliers and his advisors have more than enough help to offer, but instead they wind up like kids at those old junior high school dances, long-armed and stiff-legged, shuffling miserably around the economic dance floor. They just never learn the advantages of the opposite sex.

This is why I write and speak almost as much for the enlightenment of outsiders, who work with and depend upon the family-owned business, as I do for the members of business owning families. If we can go just a short way toward increasing the mutual understanding among all of these interdependent worlds, we will have gone a long way toward solving many of the wasteful and unnecessary failed attempts at perpetuation.

The successful family-owned business *can* continue forever. There is nothing inherent in our economic climate, our tax laws, or in government regulation that makes the environment fatal for the closely held business. Things are tough. There's no question about that. But then things always have been tough. That's what kills the start up entrepreneur, the law of the jungle. But the successful family-owned business tends to die more through neglect than homicide.

This neglected and endangered species, the family-owned business, is at the core of our society. The people who own and manage these businesses are, in general, honest, decent, God-fearing, hard working men and women who contribute immeasurable time and talent to the social and civic good. They represent, in the very best sense of the phrase, the American Dream. But the maintenance of this strong, independent, pluralistic business base requires that successful people willingly continue to risk their own money and their own guts for their own future. If the family-owned business fails, the business owner's philosophy, his freedom, and his funding disappear along with that business.

REQUIREMENTS FOR SURVIVAL

There really is no inexorable reason why the family-owned business must so often, like the mule, be limited to one-generation activity. Help *is* available, but it requires

1) *The selection and support of competent advisors ,*
2) *The contribution and discipline of committed outside directors ,*
3) *The energies of dedicated and informed managers ,*
4) *The acceptance of responsibility by competent successors, and*
5) *The education, training, and accommodation of the family .*

These requirements exist at all stages in the life of the business. They operate as much for the successors as they do for the founder. The business will change. It will grow in size, complexity and opportunity. The family itself will grow, change, and expand to encompass whole groups of people who have joined it for better or worse. But the basic requirements remain for all family-owned businesses, for all owner-managers, and for all of their heirs, relatives, advisors and associates.

There may be some excuse in the early years for the misuse of time and the lack of attention to the future. Survival is fundamental. It takes precedence in any priority system I know of. But many of our mistakes are too often allowed to take root and grow. They may be unobtrusive at first, but eventually they start coming into bloom, turning life into one damn thing after another.

These mistakes must be avoided, if possible, or at least they must be corrected--the sooner, the better. If the advisors and suppliers to new businesses are interested in more than simply charging them and selling to them, if they are interested in a long term, profitable relationship, they will go out of their way to help the founder stamp out some of the fuses he inadvertently lights in his struggle to succeed.

Later, as the business grows, the founder, his successors, his family and his managers need other kinds of help. They need practice having their decisions questioned. They need help in developing an effective organization. They need advice in how to plan. They need help learning from their mistakes. They need to know that they are not alone.

This requires something from both sides. The family managers have to realize that their business is an influential economic and social entity. Their money and power represent a new "establishment" that is increasingly recognized and accepted. But this recognition brings with it an increased responsibility to do everything possible to make sure that business *does* continue forever--and that includes willingly opening up the inner circle to the scrutiny, advice, and help of outsiders.

Professional advisors have to accept their responsibility to apply their knowledge with wisdom and understanding on the non-technical considerations unique to every family-owned business. This requires that they open their minds to accept the operation of variables in business equations which will never appear in their technical manuals.

And, finally, the major corporations, who after the family itself perhaps have the most to lose if the business fails, have to accept their responsibility to give their economic partners the same attention they give to marketing or product development. Increased sales will not solve whatever ails the closely held business, no matter how much this is true for the major corporation. In fact, increased sales will only result with any consistency once all of the other problems facing the owner-manager have been solved.

All in all, survival and perpetuation of the successful family owned business is a big order. But it can be achieved. It's achieved every day.

What I'd like to see is an increase in the number of winners.

 TWELVE COMMANDMENTS
for the
BUSINESS OWNER

1. Thou Shalt Share Thy Dream With Thy Family.

2. Thou Shalt Inform Thy Managers and Employees, "This Company Will Continue Forever."

3. Thou Shalt Develop a Workable Organization and Make It Visible on a Chart.

4. Thou Shalt Continue to Improve Thy Management Knowledge, That of Thy Managers and That of Thy Family.

5. Thou Shalt Institute an Orthodox Accounting System and Make Available the Data Therefrom to Thy Managers, Advisors, and Directors.

6. Thou Shalt Develop a Council of Competent Advisors.

7. Thou Shalt Submit Thyself to the Review of a Board of Competent Outside Directors.

8. Thou Shalt Choose Thy Successor(s).

9. Thou Shalt Be Responsible That Thy Successor(s) be Well Taught.

10. Thou Shalt Retire and Install Thy Successor(s) With Thy Powers Within Thy Lifetime.

11. Thou Canst Not Take It With Thee — So Settle Thy Estate Plans — Now.

12. Thou Shalt Apportion Thy Time to See That These Commandments Be Kept.

LÉON A. DANCO, Ph.D.
President, University Services Institute